36

W9-AXJ-309

E=MC

(63-63576) 4-22-64

Shaping a New World
MARGARET MEAD

In 1955 when Allyn Moss interviewed Margaret Mead for a magazine article on a long taxi ride to LaGuardia Airport, Miss Moss had no idea that she would one day write a book about her.

In 1954, Miss Moss became a staff writer and assistant editor for *Mademoiselle* magazine, writing among many articles one on anthropology. "It was a very happy time," she recalls, "I was being paid to spend all my time talking to anthropologists I'd read, known about, and always wanted to meet."

In 1958 she went to Italy to live and free-lance. In two years, she sold five articles—two to *Mademoiselle* (which she felt hardly counted), one to the New York *Times* (which was never published), two to European publications which paid somewhat under $20 each. "But I became a good photographer, learned Italian well enough to dream in it, and experienced enough 'cultural shock' (an expression I'd heard first from Margaret Mead) to last me all my life."

Since returning to the United States, Allyn Moss has, besides free-lancing, devoted as much time as possible to working for peace. She belongs to SANE, an organization favoring disarmament for West and East by mutual agreement.

Britannica Bookshelf—Great Lives

Shaping a New World

MARGARET MEAD

by Allyn Moss

ENCYCLOPAEDIA BRITANNICA PRESS
Chicago   New York   London

Permission to quote from Margaret Mead's works has been granted by the publishers, as follows: William Morrow & Co., Inc., Coming of Age in Samoa. Growing Up in New Guinea, From the South Seas, Male and Female, Keep Your Powder Dry, New Lives for Old, Sex and Temperament in Three Primitive Societies; *Houghton, Mifflin & Co.,* An Anthropologist at Work, *edited by Margaret Mead; Brewer, Warren & Putnam,* All True *(much of Chapter 5 is based on this work); World Publishing Company,* People and Places; *New York Academy of Sciences,* Balinese Character, A Photographic Analysis; *G. P. Putnam & Co.,* Growth and Culture, A Photographic Study of Balinese Childhood.

Permission to quote has also been granted by the publishers for excerpts from the following: *The Complete Poems of Emily Dickinson,* ed. by Thomas H. Johnson (Little, Brown and Company, 1960); Elinor Wylie, *Collected Poems* (Alfred Knopf, 1932); *The Nation,* Ruth Benedict's obituary of Franz Boas, Jan. 2, 1943; *National Parent Teachers,* "Youth Would be Valiant," October, 1941; *American Journal of Orthopsychiatry,* "Mental Health and the Wider World," January, 1962.

To my mother

TABLE OF CONTENTS

Chapter 1

"Talofa"—And So It All Began

It was boat day in Pago Pago, a lovely fall morning in 1925. Every three weeks the ship came in from Honolulu bringing mail, supplies, and produce from the United States, as well as a varying number of tourists, Navy officials, and an occasional missionary. As the S.S. *Sonoma* rounded the reef-fringed shores heading in to the sheltered harbor, the pride of the South Seas and particularly of American Samoa, cries of greeting and welcome went up from the shore—"*Talofa*," "*Talofa*," "*Talofa*."

Soon the ship was in dock and the passengers began to disembark. Among them a young, slender woman, not much over five feet tall, walked across the plank, putting her feet with determination onto the Samoan island of Tutuila, and bearing with her a most curious assortment of belongings: a Kodak Junior camera, a metal cashbox, a typewriter, a minimum of what she hoped would prove to be appropriate clothing, a delicate and hand embroidered baby pillow, $4.50

in her purse—plus the fervent hope that more money had arrived in the mail on the same ship with her—and perhaps most important of all, a strong no-nonsense look in her gray eyes.

The girl, who looked far younger than her 23 years, made her way from the boat to the one ramshackle hotel in Pago Pago, not a great distance from the harbor. This rather dilapidated palace of the tropics had been immortalized not long before by Somerset Maugham in his short story, "Miss Thompson," which later became the stage play *Rain*. Against this setting the famous Sadie Thompson had her fatal meeting with the missionary, the Reverend Davidson. And now Margaret Mead of Philadelphia, Pennsylvania—and environs—a bit queasy and weary after a voyage of 4,000 miles, had reached her first destination. She asked the hotel clerk, a shy young half-caste, if she might have a room.

Naval authorities, who had been in charge of American Samoa since 1899, had been alerted to the arrival from the United States of a Dr. Margaret Mead of Columbia University in New York City. She had, they had been informed, a fellowship grant in the biological sciences from the National Research Council, a scientific foundation. The Navy had agreed to be responsible for Dr. Mead's safety and well-being while on the islands and to help her in every way possible with her work. But they could scarcely have been prepared to find that the doctor—for Margaret Mead had completed the work for her doctor of philosophy degree at Columbia only the spring before—was a small, very young woman, come to study, of all things, the habits of adolescent girls on Samoa. And what on earth, many Navy men wondered, was an anthropologist?

Their confusion was not surprising. In 1925 few people anywhere had ever heard the word, let alone learned what it meant. But anthropology, which means—in the Greek words from which it is derived—the science of man, covers so much territory, and anthropologists do so many different things that misconceptions about both were bound to arise. Anthropologists were usually thought to be, by those with a little familiarity with the term, a group of oldish men with beards who puttered with bones in the drafty halls of museums. Actually the study of the human skeleton and the evolution of physical man is the work of physical anthropology, only one of the divisions of anthropology. Archaeologists, who are anthropologists who dig for human relics, such artifacts as tools, pottery, weapons, and so forth, and then try to put together human history that way, were always being confused with paleontologists, who study fossils of animals and plants. And ethnology, the science of cultures, the subdivision of anthropology to which Margaret Mead belonged, was continually being confused with entomology, the science of insects.

In her hotel room, complete with dilapidated mosquito netting, bamboo blinds, and an old iron bedstead, Margaret unpacked her "things." Each one had been carefully selected. (It would be no quick or easy matter to send home for anything.) The baby pillow had already served part of its purpose. Henry Crampton, a biology professor at Barnard College had said, "Take along a small pillow and you'll be able to sleep wherever you are." And he had been right, for on the *Matsonia*, the ship that took her the first 2,000 miles from San Francisco to Honolulu, she had owned no such pillow. Then, in Honolulu, her hostess, a family friend, bought her a blue silk baby pillow, exactly the kind they put in baby carriages.

Margaret Mead's metal cashbox, complete with key, was to hold the notes she would be making safe from tropical heat, seawater, rain, insect and animal life, baby hands, and curious eyes. One hundred squares of fine torn cambric were meant, in a pre-Kleenex era, for any number of emergencies— even the wiping of Samoan babies' noses—for such could be used and then thrown away. Then—besides the absolutely essential equipment: typewriter and the camera—there were photographs. Pictures of her mother, Emily Fogg Mead, who was herself a sociologist; of her father, Edward Sherwood Mead, a professor at the University of Pennsylvania, who, realizing that Margaret's grant was not enough to cover her travelling expenses, had insisted on paying them himself— $1,000—because he felt "adding to the sum of exact knowledge in the world was the one thing in life most worth doing." Pictures of her brothers and her sisters, of friends from childhood and from college.

The photographs were important, not only to help combat possible homesickness and to keep those she loved close to her, but because she knew that in the human encounters she would make with Samoans proud of their children and their relatives, she would have something of her own to show them—people in her life that would help make her existence and background, though far away and remote, none the less real and personal.

Of the few books Margaret had brought with her, the one she valued most was an anthology of poetry Ruth Benedict, her teacher and dear friend, had typed for her, carefully choosing poems she herself loved and felt sure would become equally dear to Margaret. Dr. Benedict, a brilliant and outstanding anthropologist whose later sensitive analysis of the patterns of culture among various American Indian tribes

was inspiration to M.

[12]

has never been surpassed, was also a fine poet. And Margaret, whose own childhood and life had been filled with poetry, found in Ruth Benedict, despite the differences in their ages, a truly kindred spirit. Among the poems, one by Emily Dickinson had already become a favorite:

> I never saw a Moor—
> I never saw the Sea—
> Yet know I how the Heather looks
> And what a Billow be.
>
> I never spoke with God
> Nor visited in Heaven—
> Yet certain am I of the spot
> As if the checks were given.

And so, although she was over 7,000 miles from home, family, and friends, in a day when planes did not yet fly across oceans and transcontinental phone calls were not yet a reality, Margaret was alone—and yet, not quite alone.

The few letters of introduction she had with her proved to be critically helpful, particularly one to the head of the Medical Services on Samoa, who saw that the nurses helped her. The chief Samoan nurse at the hospital in Pago Pago, G. F. Pepe—whose name could be translated as Butterfly— agreed to start Margaret in her study of the Samoan language. Each day the chief nurse came to visit Margaret in her hotel room, and for one hour every day Margaret listened to Pepe's gentle voice and tried to capture the feeling of the soft liquid language she had to learn before she could even begin her work. First Pepe taught her the phrases and greetings of courtesy that are so commonly used and so important among the Samoans. *"Talofa,"* Margaret intoned in imitation of Pepe. *"Talofa lava,"* replied Pepe for this was the proper response and meant, "Love to thee, indeed." If Pepe asked Margaret, *"Malolo?"* Margaret soon knew the courteous answer, *"Malolo fu'afetai"* ("I am rested, thanks to thee.") And she was also able to say the most beautiful expression one Samoan says to another after twilight, *"Tofa. Tofa soi fua,"* which means "Sleep thou. Sleep and life to thee."

It was difficult to pronounce the almost totally different sounds of a non-European language, although the vowels in Samoan were said almost exactly as they are in Italian, which helped. The old spelling, Pango Pango, more accurately represents the pronounciation than Pago Pago, g in Samoan always being pronounced ng. But knowing where to put the accent was tricky. She was sure, for instance, that she had been saying, on the occasions when she dared to practice her new language on Samoans other than Pepe, "The Samoan language is very difficult," and had been puzzled when her listeners had regarded her with no more than a blank eye of confusion. When she discovered that she had actually been saying, "The Samoan language is very vaccination," she became more determined than ever to master the subtle rules of when to place the accent on the second syllable, and when to put it on the third—for that was what made all the difference. Then there was Samoan grammar—unfamiliar and strange—for nouns became verbs and verbs nouns in the most amazing manner. All of this meant that for the one hour Pepe came each day to teach Margaret new words and phrases and rules of the island language, Margaret felt she had to work at least another seven hours by herself. For she could see no point even in going out into the streets of Pago Pago, let alone on into the villages of

Samoa, until she was ready to speak, to be understood, and above all to understand fully what was being said.

This was a tense time for Margaret. There were days she doubted her ability to learn the language as well as she needed to. She found herself saying, "I can't do it. I can't do it." Weeks passed. One afternoon she caught herself saying it again—"I can't do it"—except now she was saying it in Samoan, and she began to believe she could do it after all. Still there was so much to do before she could really begin. The fellowship grant was paid to her in installments and only two months in advance. The hotel food was not always of the best. A sad-eyed cook named *Fa'a lavelave* (Misfortune) introduced Margaret to her first contact with some bad *Papalangi* food (the Samoan word for white man's cooking), but he also served some very good Samoan dishes. Coconut and bread-fruit, especially when baked, were delicious. Fish and chicken Samoan style could be eaten with relish. But taro, a potato-like root much eaten in the islands, tasted to her like Ivory soap, and pork native-style was so slightly cooked that she resolved to tell Samoans she could not eat it because of a personal family taboo, an excuse she knew they would accept since traditionally Samoans had their own taboos to observe. She was glad that for the most part she found Samoan food highly edible, not only because she would be living on native foods for many months, but because she knew it would be highly insulting to her Samoan hosts if she were not to obviously enjoy whatever fare they served her. An anthropologist who offends the sensitivities of the people he has come to know might as well take the next ship home.

The weeks passed. Margaret, almost prepared now to do her job, grew restless. It was hard to remain in Pago Pago— in Samoa and yet not in Samoa—for the harbor town was more

U.S. Navy than Samoan. She was still only on the fringes of the work she had come to do. There was no one in Samoa with whom she could discuss the problems before her. Navy officials found it hard to understand her mission. Shocked at the idea of her going alone into the Samoan villages, the officials laid down various rules for her safety, some of which she had to observe. They gave her warnings about native discomforts that she would have to endure—the Samoan habit, for instance of eating rotten fish. This seemed a silly warning and it was. For when she finally tried rotten fish, she found it delicious and learned that to the Samoans the dish was a delicacy in the same way the expensive rotting cheeses Westerners like so much—Camembert, Roquefort, blue—are. To her own astonishment, as she later recalled, she was "always tempted to take one more bit to be sure it was rotten."

At last, after six weeks, Margaret felt she was ready for her first major Samoan encounter. A half-caste woman who dressed with a mixture of Parisian chic and South Sea Island charm and who spoke tolerable English took Margaret round the coast to Vaitogi, known as the Village of the Turtle and the Shark to meet Chief Ufuti, a relative of hers. First impressions are vivid. As they approached, Margaret remembers seeing "the Village of the Turtle and the Shark lying still and clear in the hot sun—the houses with thatched beehive-shaped roofs and no walls at all, only wooden pillars, were scattered about the village under the breadfruit trees." She was amazed at how everything seemed low on the ground. Chief Ufuti received the two women in his dwelling house, which was set in a grove of palm trees. Now the crucial test was at hand. As Margaret entered the chief's house she carefully prepared to say the words Butterfly had taught her which were proper Samoan etiquette for such an occasion.

"May you most honorable enter," said Chief Ufuti.

"I have humbly come saving the presence of your Lordship and her who sits in the back of the house," answered Margaret. (This last referred to the Chief's wife.)

"Alas for the coming of your Ladyship," Chief Ufuti continued, "there is nothing good in the house."

And then, to complete this polite dialogue, Margaret remembered the last of her carefully memorized phrases— "Oh let the matter rest. It is of no consequence whatsoever."

Clearly, from the kind look in Chief Ufuti's eyes, from the warmth she felt from every member of his family, Margaret had passed the test. Fresh coconut was served and everyone drank the juice with murmurs of thanks. Soon Margaret's chaperone went back to the port and left her alone with Chief Ufuti and his family, which was, she was told, now also her own family. The sun sank down to the sea. And so it all began—

Chapter 2

Pennsylvania Childhood

Who was this girl who seemed so unafraid of life in all its variety and strangeness? What kind of young woman was it who could drop old habits and comforts, leave friends and family many thousands of miles away, eat never-before-tasted foods, adopt new ways, learn difficult native skills and a totally different language in a matter of weeks? Above all where had she acquired the rare and special talent of reaching out to unknown peoples whose entire way of living contrasted greatly with her own but with whom nonetheless she was able to find and share a common ground—that of humanness? What made this person the way she was? Who was Margaret Mead?

These were questions many people would be asking a few years later when Margaret Mead had returned from the South Seas and when her first book, *Coming of Age in Samoa* came out in 1928 to startle a good part of the American reading public and a number of social scientists with its lucidity, intelligence, literary style, scientific soundness, and courage.

For though she was only 26 years old when the book was published, she had not been afraid to write strongly and to draw conclusions from her subject matter. But surprising as she may have seemed to many people, young as she was to have written so wisely (a few readers assumed the book had been written by a very old lady), Margaret Mead was no surprise to those who knew her; for she grew as logically and soundly out of her own background and upbringing as a sunflower might out of rich earth well watered and beneath a profusion of sunlight.

Margaret did not come from what would have been called in those days, or, for that matter now, an average American home. Born December 16, 1901, in Philadelphia, Pennsylvania, of a father who was an economics professor and a mother who worked as a sociologist while raising a family of five children, Margaret was brought up to think, and to watch —and to be watched. She was, as she put it, "a notebook child." Her mother recorded her questions and her comments, and Margaret liked it. When she was still quite little, her mother was making a study of Italian immigrant families. The Meads lived then in the midst of the Italian neighborhood in Hammonton, New Jersey. Her mother put her on the scale to compare her weight with that of the Italian children. She was taken to a big Italian wedding. She played with Italian children, but she never thought of them as "immigrants"—as most of the community did—but just as other people.

A few years later, when Margaret was nine, her paternal grandmother, Mrs. Martha Ramsey Mead, helped change Margaret from one of the observed to one of the observers. Margaret had a little sister, Elizabeth, who was three, and a baby sister, Priscilla, just beginning to talk. Grandmother Mead, herself a teacher and firm believer in progressive education, asked Margaret to jot down all the new words in her sisters' vocabulary, and to try and figure out which songs, stories, or nursery rhymes the new words came from. Margaret came up with all sorts of sources. She traced the word "raggedy," which the baby was using, to James Whitcomb Riley's poem that began:

> *O the Raggedy Man! He works fer Pa;*
> *An' he's the goodest man ever you saw!*

Grandmother Mead remained a strong influence in Margaret's early life. Her grandmother had graduated from a teachers college with her husband after they were married. When he died she took his place as principal of a high school. Later on she taught primary school, and then, when her son Edward married, she went to live with him and his family. This not only helped free Margaret's mother to go on with some of her sociological work but provided Margaret with a wonderful tutor, a most important addition; for the Meads were highly skeptical of the kind of education Margaret would get at the local schools where memorization, dull routine, and many second-rate teaching materials were the rule. Besides, what with frequent moving and a winter of whooping cough that once kept Margaret out of school for a whole long year, much of her formal education was conducted at home where she learned algebra before arithmetic and botany before spelling in accord with Grandmother Mead's progressive methods, which were far ahead of their time. Whenever Margaret did go back to school, she was never behind the rest of her class.

So the idea of women who worked and of women who thought about and did important things was hardly strange even to the very young Margaret Mead. It just seemed natural to her that a woman did some kind of work in addition to marrying and having a family and bringing up children. To most people in the United States at the beginning of the twentieth century, however, it was not at all natural for a woman to bring up a family *and* work. The battle for woman suffrage was coming to its climax—Margaret's mother was a vigorous suffragette—and woman's place was supposed to be most definitely not only *in* the home, but *in* the kitchen and the nursery, and not in the study or at the library desk, where Margaret's mother spent the late evening hours working on her own civic activities or proofreading for her husband, who wrote many books on finance. Though the Meads were aware of the prevalent attitudes towards women who did anything more intelligent than housework or waiting on tables, they were hardly disturbed by it. Professor Mead not only respected and encouraged his wife's work, but two of the Meads' changes of residence were made to correspond with Mrs. Mead's needs to be near the groups of Italians she was studying. The various towns and suburbs they settled in, though, were always within commuting distance of the University of Pennsylvania, where Professor Mead taught.

That Margaret's family moved often during her childhood was to be of great help in her later life as an anthropologist. Always new homes, new parts of the country, new furniture, different kinds of beds to sleep in, new friends to make, new games to learn, new roads to walk—adjusting to changes soon became natural to Margaret. The Meads lived first on one side of Philadelphia, then on another. For a long time, till Margaret was nine, a big house in Hammonton, New Jersey, the little town where they lived surrounded by the

Italians Mrs. Mead was studying, was home. There a high evergreen hedge separated the family from the town, and five acres of land gave the children the feeling of a separate world —two acres were blueberry patch crosshatched by paths that Margaret gave names to. But later they lived in Lansdowne and in Swarthmore, suburbs of Philadelphia, and at other times during Margaret's childhood before she was ten, they moved into rented furnished houses in the city in winter and went to the seashore or to the mountains in summer. Margaret *had* to be flexible, her roots the kind she could carry inside of her and take with her wherever she went.

Curiosity about the world, all of it, belief in the power of knowledge, respect for each individual—these attitudes that she inherited from her parents and their parents were part of the portable equipment that never left her, no matter how many times she moved. The things she learned to do at home from her mother and her grandmother were also part of that equipment, for those were things she could do anywhere. Her grandmother was determined to make her into a good botanist, and wherever the Meads moved Margaret had to make a collection of pressed flowers. She remembers ". . . dipping the blossoms in alum to keep the color, or sometimes making blueprints of them to show the outlines of the form. In each place we explored what was there, hard, watching for the birds, collecting the flowers, and when mother could find someone, being taught something special—basketry, woodwork, carving, weaving."

Each new move meant Margaret had to make new friends. Since most children are suspicious of newcomers, Margaret had begun to collect all sorts of new games so she could offer the new children variations on their old games. She also had a col-

[23]

lection of ideas of things to do. This made it much easier for her to make friends. But she knew, even if perhaps they didn't, that she wasn't actually inventing new games or things to do, but instead she was making versions of what she had seen or learned somewhere else. When she was seven she saw a play some neighboring children had composed, and later she made another version. She was very much aware when, for instance, she made up a play and put a song in it from a song book she'd seen somewhere, that she was putting it together, and not making it up entirely.

This ability to make a patchwork quilt out of the colorful fragments of Margaret's diversified childhood continued, and at some point she discovered that lists somehow made it easier for her to put everything in some kind of order. She kept lists of all the houses she'd lived in, of all the contagious diseases she and her brother and sisters had had, how old they were, what year it was, of all the cooks who'd come and gone—who went pretty often "because my mother worried so much about treating them fairly that she rather overwhelmed them with discussions of their rights." But all these lists kept Margaret, she later recalled, ". . . very conscious of just where I was, just what day it was, just how old I was. I could go back in my mind and say: yes, that was the summer that we lived in the Swain house in Nantucket, and I heard that story the day we stopped to eat thick peach ice cream in a little ice cream parlor right next to the house where the nasturtiums came through the fence."

But when Margaret was ten, life settled down a bit for the Meads. The family bought a big farm in Bucks County, Pennsylvania, which had been a station on the underground railway during slavery days, and for four years they stayed on there.

[24]

Margaret's world now included 107 acres of land two wells, and two houses to explore—their own which had 18 rooms, a milk cellar, and a kitchen with six doors; and the house the farmer, who cultivated mixed crops on the farm, lived in. There was also a wonderful three-story barn. The children used the loft at the top to give plays in, and when they played hide-and-seek they could jump down the chute through which the hay for the horses was pitched. There was a brook, too, and a ravine. Sometimes Margaret staged plays she wrote there, too, for she was fascinated by everything that had to do with the theater. She had cast her first play at seven. (Her maternal grandmother, she remembers, called her "a tiresome child who was always writing long plays nobody wanted to listen to.") And at 20 she put on an outdoor pageant, which was a huge success except that so many of the children came down with poison ivy afterwards they had to postpone the opening of school for a week.

Life in the Buckingham Valley was full for Margaret. She got to know each individual member of the community, who lived in every house, and all the rumors and half-understood stories about what went on in the different lonely farms. Later on in college she would try to write short stories that might explain some of the strange and violent behavior of these people: a man who beat his wife with his son's train of cars and then, when the baby was born, gave everybody in the country store cigars; the man who shot his niece and hid for days while all the men in the county hunted for him, and then sent them notes telling them where he'd been—just under that bridge when they went over it.

She soon knew every road and every stick and tree and turning on them—down the three quarters of a mile of dirt road

[25]

to the little store, along the turnpike in each direction to the two slightly less tiny towns where she went to school. One way led to the Buckingham Friends School in Lahaska, which she attended for two years, 1913 till 1915, and the other to Buckingham High School, where she started in 1915—and a third, straight down another mile to the lonely little station where her father arrived in a slow, dirty, little train and someone in the family met him in a horse and buggy to drive him home.

There seemed, to Margaret, as she remembers them, to be so much more time in those years. "Time to do things that one thought up oneself. Time to read hundreds of books a year—every book in the school library, then every book in the public library, and every magazine allowed and forbidden that came into the house. Time to learn poetry. You could practice it walking to and from school, sloshing through the snow in winter, toiling through the heat in the hot June, and muttering little pieces to match the weather.

> *The sun that brief December day,*
> *Rose cheerless over hills of gray,*
> *And, darkly circled, gave at noon*
> *A sadder light than waning moon.*

Or

> *'Long about knee-deep in June,*
> *'Bout the time strawberries melts*
> *On the vine. . . .*

There was time to play. Margaret organized a group of 12 children who lived in the Valley, six boys and six girls, and they called themselves the Buckingham Climbers Club. They were a very mixed group of children. Margaret remembers, "Their parents ranged from a professor and a banker to farm-

she always lead in something

[26]

ers and farmhands, some were bright and some stupid but it was necessary to have that many to do the things we wanted to do—so we fitted ourselves together and made the best of the differences among us." Later, when Margaret Mead had to live with and get along with all kinds of people—not only primitive people, but Americans, Australians, Britishers who worked as patrol officers, doctors, enlisted men, admirals, governors, missionaries on the fringes of civilization—this ability to make friends, to trust, to put up with strange attitudes and habits of speech that Margaret first developed in the scattered countryside of the Buckingham Valley stood her in good stead. The B. C. C., as they called the club, met at each other's houses, gave recitations, played such active outdoor games as run sheepy run, debated who was greater, Washington or Lincoln.

In Margaret's private imagination, always vivid, a group of daydreams in which she would be carried off by pirates or robbers or the Germans held the center of the stage during these years. But what was important in all her imaginings was that she would get the chance to learn and speak many languages. Sometimes she also would imagine learning to paint and sing and dance—things she despaired of ever having the time to learn at home or really at all. But—and this too was crucial—eventually she would come back home and be recognized by her family as herself. The idea of learning many languages remained with her. She was always seeking out children who spoke or whose parents spoke foreign languages. In high school she knew a Jewish girl whose father was a shoemaker who knew ten languages.

Meanwhile things that affected everyone were happening in the real world outside the Buckingham Valley. The Meads, who felt strongly about all injustice, felt themselves involved in many national and international issues. There was a very old Negro man who had been a slave before the Civil War and who had reached safety in the Buckingham Valley. He had a very young wife, and Margaret's mother always had the children address her as "Mrs." even though most of the local people laughed at this. Margaret's grandmother explained carefully to the children "that we were all children of God, but she did say when I came in with my hair flying that I looked like 'the Wild Man of Borneo.' . . . It never occurred to her that I might ever meet anyone like the Wild Man of Borneo and so should learn to treat him with respect."

Margaret's mother was actively engaged in the struggle to get women the right to vote. People in the community knew it. Once someone sent the family a valentine. A drawing showed a row of neat children with shining faces and the text read: "We have plenty to eat you bet—Our mother ain't no suffragette."

So, at home, Margaret learned from what she later described as her mother's "indignations and enthusiasms" and from her grandmother's "careful compassion for plants and baby chicks and children and strangers . . . that there were many wrongs to be righted in the world. . . . Somewhere in the big cities there were things called 'sweat shops' where women worked under 'terrible conditions.' Citizens had organized a kind of union called the Consumers League to demand that the things they bought should have labels saying they weren't made in sweat shops. Then there were many many people who didn't have clothes for their children, and there was something called The Needlework Guild to which people brought handmade clothing, always in pairs—two little sacks, two little dresses, so that our dining room looked as if all clothes were twins. There were people who were starving, and who had to be fed; there were terrible injustices to members of other races and religions—and to women who weren't allowed to vote. There was corruption in politics, which was one reason our schools were bad. And there was perhaps most of all ignorance. . . ."

Then there was the war. At first the "great war for civilization," as World War I was called, which began in 1914 and which the United States entered in 1917, seemed very far away. Then tales of the "rape of Belgium" floated into the Pennsylvania valleys, and Margaret used to imagine the German armies marching through the Pennsylvania wheat fields. War movies too made deep impressions on a mind as awake and sensitive as Margaret's. When she graduated from the Buckingham Friends School in 1915, she read a graduating essay titled "If Germany Had . . ." on a stage decorated with great red poppies.

More and more as Margaret Mead grew older and more conscious of these human and social problems that kept people enslaved, or at war, or in misery, she felt a need to put her own opinions and ideas into words—to write things or to say things seemed terribly important.

There were endless opportunities to recite, and Margaret rarely missed one. At school and club, on holidays, there were chances to recite old poems and new pieces. Margaret's father, who detested what he called "the lawn sprinkler method of public speaking—just spraying looks in every direction without ever meeting anyone's eyes," used to come and sit in the front row and *make* Margaret look him in the eye. In turn she remembers flustering him, "When I'd get a line wrong and he'd look apprehensive, and then I'd triumphantly make up a new line so it would rhyme safely after all." Later, in high school, she made four-minute speeches for war causes; in college she debated; and even in Samoa, where she had to learn to make replies to the flowery speeches that are part of Samoan etiquette, this talent for speaking proved important.

Her ability to memorize and remember all sorts of miscellaneous things was so good her mother was sometimes irritated by it. Margaret was able to store any amount of "nonsense and trivia" in the accessible parts of her mind—but she was also able to forget it quickly once she had no more need for it. This skill was invaluable when in school cramming for examinations. She could quickly assimilate the material, she recalls, "trade routes to Hongkong and Odessa, dates, the capital of Maine 'on the Kennebec River,' how to spell phthisic—a great clutter of stuff, each fact unrelated to the next, organized for a day or a week, could then be quietly returned to the dictionaries and geography books from which it came. . . ." And later on in her life, this capacity helped again when she arrived in a new native village with hundreds of new names and places and things that had to be learned by rote and that all sounded like nonsense in the beginning.

But it was writing that mattered most. Writing was lasting. Through writing one might change people's attitudes, one might pass on traditions of freedom and justice that uphold human dignity. A man might die, might be destroyed, but his ideas would live on if he had set them down on paper. It was natural for Margaret to write. Almost every member of the Mead family did. Her father, of course, wrote books on economics and finance. Her mother wrote essays and all sorts of sociological papers. Margaret began writing verse when she was very young.

When she was about 13, she began to write papers for some women who belonged to a women's club and who didn't know how to write their own. She remembers reporting lectures which were given at "the travelling Lyceum that came in winter and gave lectures and entertainments up in the second floor of an old rickety meeting building" for the county newspaper. Later in high school—*another* high school in Doylestown, Pennsylvania, which she attended from 1916 to 1918—she wrote an account of a class trip for a local newspaper and got paid for it. In the same high school she helped start the school magazine, which was printed in the local newspaper shop. Taking the copy down and waiting for proof gave her some idea about the whole process of editing and publishing. And all the time she was learning to analyze language—"to wonder and experiment with figures of speech," as she later said.

Reading was another way of learning about writing. Margaret read continually from her early childhood on. She even read books she was forbidden to read—all kinds of "series" like the Alger books; the Motor Boat Boys on Nantucket, in the Everglades; the Grammar School boys. Margaret's mother greatly disapproved of "series." She pronounced the word, Margaret remembers, "as if it were a form of crime against the human mind," and she made it clear to Margaret that there was bad writing as well as good writing, writing by people who were not great writers but who just "happened to write books." So when Margaret read "forbidden books," she did so in a very special way, trying to understand, at the same time that she enjoyed many of them, what it was about them that made them "bad." By reading cheap, shoddy work with this sort of critical attention, Margaret became sensitive not only to literary quality, but she also learned a lot about the kind of writing that appeals to most people, and about what subjects meant most to the mass of Americans, the nonintellectuals. Her observations of this last kind of writing and her own natural inclinations to remain part of the people—and not just a part of any special segment of them—made her, years later when she was writing many books and articles for a mass audience that rare phenomenon: a scientist who was not only able to write simply and dramatically, but one without contempt for mass media, without snobbery about the public; a highly intelligent human being who felt it to be her responsibility to communicate even the most complicated scientific findings in a clear and down-to-earth way, so that everyone who might be interested would be able to understand them.

Books, of course, were to young Margaret much more than a way of learning to write. The people who lived in them were real to her—a part of her life, a reminder of all the amazing things that might happen to one. Especially exciting, as Margaret later said, were all the brave and romantic women "like Joan of Arc, and Sappho the Greek poet, and Elizabeth Barrett Browning who had been turned into an invalid by a tyrannous father till Robert Browning came and rescued her. There was Saint Elizabeth who had been caught feeding the poor and said she had an apron full of roses, and lo when she opened her apron it *was* full of roses. There was Jo in *Little Women* who turned into a woman who ran a school. . . ."

Then there were the women who wrote books and of whom Margaret became increasingly conscious. Louisa May Alcott, who wrote *Little Women;* Harriet Beecher Stowe, who had helped to free the slaves by writing *Uncle Tom's Cabin;* and George Eliot (who was really named Marian Evans); and Charlotte Bronte, who along with her famous sisters, Emily and Anne, had all had to use men's names as pseudonyms to get their books accepted. "But that was a long time ago," she later recalled. Now, Margaret knew, "One could be a writer and sign a woman's name if one wanted to."

Or, for that matter, Margaret realized, as she watched the women who in one way or another came into her life, a woman could do almost anything she chose to do. She could be a home economics teacher *and* a librarian *and,* as she later became, a copy editor like her Aunt Isabel, who lived in Brooklyn and who was also a skilled linguist. (Margaret sometimes went to visit her, and then they went into Manhattan to the theater.) A woman might be an art teacher like Pemberton Ginther, who lived near Lahaska across the Buckingham Valley, and who gave Margaret drawing lessons. Pemberton Ginther also wrote and illustrated the Beth Ann series of children's books. Sometimes she had Margaret pose for the illustrations. One could be like Margaret's music teacher, who had to work hard because her husband was an elderly scholar who didn't know how to make a living; or one could be like the ministers' wives and daughters who lived in the rectory and helped run the parish. Or one might choose not to marry—perhaps end up like the two unmarried school teachers Margaret knew whose fiancés had died. *She learned that she had the oppor. to do anything.*

So as a girl growing up, Margaret had a sense of freedom that was very rare in those days, or even today. She really believed that a young woman might *choose* what she wanted to do. She felt there were "all sorts of possibilities," and that these depended on what one wanted to do, and what talents one might have. At different times, she remembers, she wanted to be different things—"a nun and a lawyer and a minister's wife —to have six children." They all seemed to her quite practical ambitions that could be talked about. She felt no limitations. Before her lay a magnificent open vista called life. She was sure of it, for wasn't it already growing and expanding within her?

Chapter 3

Search

Margaret's high school years were as varied as her earlier one's had been. Between 1914 and 1918 she went to four different high schools. First she attended the Buckingham Friends School, a three year school (8th grade and two years of high school) taught in one room by one teacher. Margaret's school books were two generations old and her Latin grammar was the same one her grandmother had studied Latin from. Next, a year in a new three-year high school with the same teacher and a new principal. The teachers, Margaret remembers, were "hopelessly inadequate even for the text books they used."

Margaret transferred to Doylestown in 1918. This was a four-year high school that was soon to feel the effects of World War I. The chemistry teacher was drafted and his place was taken by a grade school teacher who, Margaret recalls, "was never quite sure what gas the students had succeeded in making." Because Margaret was good in chemistry, the teacher marked the other students' papers by Margaret's, a practice that was not much help to Margaret herself. German had been discontinued because of the war, and this meant that Margaret took four years of Latin but missed the required second language. Civics and American history were taught by the principal, a man of Italian descent who brought the enthusiasm of the convinced and proud new American to his teaching.

Margaret's high school years were very much colored by the war. She organized a group of young people her own age who, as she later said, "met and danced holes in the carpet of my parents' rented house—or in Lent played games instead." The older college boys she knew were already in the Army; and she spent the summer of 1918, a year after she graduated from high school, as she recalls, "cooking on wartime rations for a household of eight (servants had disappeared and wheat flour was scarce) and knitting sox while I read aloud from wartime memoirs to my two grandmothers."

In the autumn of 1918 the whole family moved to New Hope so that Margaret could have a year of college preparatory French to get ready for Wellesley, which had been her mother's first college. The school in New Hope was private and just for girls. There, surrounded by elaborately reconstructed barns and pig pens, which had been made over into houses and classrooms (there were only 13 pupils and 5 teachers in all), she took three years of French in one with a "*grande dame*" in her middle 70's, who had once been a friend of Robert Louis Stevenson. There also, as well as at home, she did housework. All of this meant that by the end of the war, Margaret was essentially grown-up. It also meant that she never belonged to the postwar flapper generation. Already her sights and the sights of the young men she and her friends knew were set on the work they meant to do—after the war. Margaret, however, was still not quite sure what she wanted to do with her life. She intended to major in English, a natural enough choice since so many of her gifts lay in that direction. She had always been able to write easily and on order. Literature and the theater were deep lifetime loves. Her head was, in her own words, "stuffed with the words in which experience had been phrased by the greatest writers of English," and one of her friends once told her she'd never be able to write because her head and her conversation was such a welter of quotations.

But she knew that there were many other things she could do as well, things to which she was also strongly attracted. She was interested in languages. She had a feeling for theater. She had a gift for organizing. She felt keenly about the need to take an active part in the world, and to help eliminate misery and injustice and ignorance. She had been trained to think scientifically. She was awfully good with her hands. She could make baskets, model in clay, design any number of contraptions. She had taken drawing lessons since she was seven and by the time she was thirteen she had completed the "customary exercises" —drawing white cubes and spheres and cones and plaster casts in charcoal. She had begun to work in oils and considered the possibility of becoming a painter.

Still she had no idea of just how she was going to make her contribution to the world, or in what direction her road would ultimately lead.

How does a human being, aware of infinite choice, come to a point of commitment—to that ability to say "Yes" not to everything, but to some thing or some things that seem to belong to him more than the others. Many years later, when Margaret Mead had already written many books and was known throughout the world, she was asked to try to remember the events, the influences, the "moments of personal discovery" that led her to make the decisions she did and to have the strong convictions she came to have. Most important among these was a deep sense of responsibility that belongs, she believed, "to anyone who cares about our arts and sciences" and a consciousness of tradition and the need to pass these on.

First she remembered a book, by Charles Carleton Coffin, *The Story of Liberty*, in which there was a chapter about John Wyclif. It told how a group of monks at Runnymede in England were so disturbed by Wyclif's teachings that they dug up his bones and scattered his ashes in a brook. But still they could not stop him, for his writings spread his words to other parts of the world, and in that way he became, as the title of the chapter called him: "The Man Who Preached After He Was Dead."

It suddenly seemed true and terribly important to Margaret that by writing things down one could pass on a tradition, a great idea—and in that way become part of something much bigger and more lasting than one's self. How wonderful that would be.

Years later, in high school she wrote a class poem. It began with practically every name she could fit into a rather imperfect meter, virtually all the poets and saints and sages she could think of. John Wyclif was stuck in among Dante and Virgil and Joan of Arc and Sappho—because he stood for a particular point—as she said later, "for the abidingness of the written word, and the way tradition was passed on." The last part of the poem went like this:

> *On your shoulders falls their mantle*
> *Settling light as a caress.*
> *Will you answer, heirs of ages?*
> *"Saints and Sages—we say yes!"*

Looking back, she asks herself: "Where had I got the notion that the burden which was to be taken so seriously was light?" For it seemed strange to think of a burden—in this case the tradition of ages— as light. At first the answer escaped her—and especially the line "Settling light as a caress" was puzzling. Was it a contradiction? Another poem provided the answer.

Somewhere in her earlier childhood, Margaret, like most of the English-speaking children in every part of the world had learned this poem of Robert Louis Stevenson.

> Dark brown is the river,
> Golden is the sand.
> It flows along for ever
> With trees on either hand.

> Green leaves a-floating,
> Castles of the foam,
> Boats of mine a-boating—
> Where will all come home?

> On goes the river
> And out past the mill,
> Away down the valley,
> Away down the hill.

> Away down the river,
> A hundred miles or more,
> Other little children
> Shall bring my boats ashore.

It was the images of the second stanza—the boats that were only light green leaves, "castles on the foam," that were crucial for her. Because "it was the great fragility of tradition coupled with the certainty that, nevertheless,

> *Away down the river,*
> *A hundred miles or more,*
> *Other little children*
> *Shall bring my boats ashore."*

So, while the castles *were* on the foam and the boats were only leaves, there was a sharing of the burdens, and the children down the river were there "to lighten the load on our shoulders." Still, she could never quite forget how very fragile and delicate the castles and the boats were.

A sense of religion also played an important part in helping to form Margaret's feelings of commitment and dedication to work, to life. Though the Meads were not regularly church-going, religion was strong in the family background Margaret's mother's family were Unitarian, her father's were Methodist. Margaret's ancestors who came from the British Isles had been Dissenters. Some, she was told, were known as Covenanters and had hidden in caves in Scotland to escape their religious enemies. Some had come to Massachusetts Bay in 1628. Her great-great grandfather had been a circuit-riding pastor, and her great uncle was a leading Methodist minister of his day. On her mother's side there was an ancestor who had been read out of the Unitarian Church. And there was even a great-uncle who had been a Mohammedan—or Muslim as they are called today.

With this much individuality in the family's religious history, it is only to be expected that Margaret's parents and her grandmother (who did attend a church) would leave it completely up to Margaret to choose whatever kind of religious training she might want. Margaret began looking for a church of her liking when she was five or six years old. First she went to a Presbyterian Sunday school. Then, when her family moved to Swarthmore, Pennsylvania, she went to Quaker Meeting. Most of the neighbor children were Friends, members of the Quaker faith. She remembers clinging to the Quaker meetinghouse window with a group of her friends to watch a wedding.

When the Mead family moved into the Buckingham Valley, Margaret transferred to the Quaker Meeting there, which was very small. But when, about this time, the Episcopal rector, Mr. Bell, and his daughter, came to call on the Meads, Margaret moved her chair over beside his to ask him if she could become a member of his church, Trinity Church in the town of Buckingham, which to this day she considers as her own parish. This choice was completely Margaret's own; she made this decision because, after attending so many other churches, she realized that she liked the ritual and the style and all the English historical and religious tradition associated with that particular church.

At home, there was no regular Bible-reading period, but Margaret's father was thoroughly steeped in the Book and quoted it constantly. As she recalls, she recognized that, "There were Biblical cadences beneath the sentences in his books on economics." Margaret's mother did at one time have the Bible read to the children, and she even had Margaret read it in German because she thought it would be good for her "to have to confront the Bible in another language." Of course she also learned Scriptures in the Episcopal church and in school; children were expected to memorize passages from the Bible as they were expected to memorize so many other things. The 23rd Psalm and 13th Corinthians were engraved on her brain. But two Biblical themes in particular added vividly to Margaret's ideas about responsibility and the need for each person to give what he could to the world.

The parable of the "talents" and the "exceedingly wicked man" (for so he seemed to Margaret) who wrapped his one talent that his lord had given to him in a napkin, and did nothing about it except to bring it out again (Luke xix, 20) made a very deep impression. Whenever Margaret heard that story, she thought at once that the word "talent," which in the parable referred, of course, to a coin, also referred to the *talents* an individual possessed. And, as she came from a family that she remembers, "scarcely mentioned taxes except to say that they were not heavy enough to improve the schools as they ought to be improved," it never occurred to Margaret that the literal meaning of the word "talent" as it was used in the parable only had to do with money. For to Margaret, "people who did not use money responsibly and people who did not use their abilities to sing and write books" were the same as "people who put their talents in napkins," and they were "very wicked" because of it. Then, besides her feeling that "the man who, having only one talent, had left it in a napkin and done nothing further about it had done something very wrong," this sin somehow got mixed up in her mind with "the sin against the Holy Ghost, the unforgivable sin that no one could explain to you and that you might commit therefore no matter how good you were."

Margaret felt this obligation "laid on each individual to use whatever gifts he had," even though she was not yet sure what her own most fruitful gifts were. So she continued to develop them all in faith that a time would come when she would *know* which of her own "talents" not to bury in the ground. At the same time, she never forgot the fragility of human tradition and culture, and how, some day, as in the Stevenson poem, there was the dreadful possibility that those boats might *not* be brought ashore.

She knew, of course, that the education she had received in the arts and sciences from her parents and from the books she had read had made her a bearer of this tradition. And she knew that, as a bearer of this tradition, all the things she had learned to think and to understand and to do were actually a precious legacy left to her by many great scientists and writers and artists of the past. Therefore, she felt, it was her task—as it was the task of all the men and women in the world who cared—not only to pass on this wonderful accumulation of wisdom but to add to it as well.

As she grew older, Margaret Mead turned more and more to this question of how she herself might best succeed in passing this tradition on to future generations. Was the writing of books, she wondered, the best way, the only way to communicate these teachings? What about people? Why was it that the impression made by one human being on another was often the most lasting, the strongest sort of contact? When she was in college she saw a play on the New York stage called *The Inheritors*. In this play, as Margaret remembers it, an old grandmother speaking from pioneer days tells about a time when her whole family was away from home and another pioneer family, passing by in a covered wagon, stopped over, the way people did in those days when they found an empty house. She recalls "they lived in the house for two or three days and went away again without ever having been seen by the people whose unwitting guests they had been. And the old grandmother said something like this: 'And she baked a loaf of brown bread and left it there, and it didn't taste like any bread I'd ever eaten. They must have been some kind of foreign people who had a recipe that was different from any we ever had. I used to experiment and try to make that loaf of bread, but I never could. I always hoped some day I'd meet that woman and she'd tell me how.' " That play added another element to the picture of the fragility of human tradition that continued to make such a profound impression on Margaret, and she was joining one idea to another. For instance, she realized, "It is not only that books live, even though their authors may have been burned; it is also that if the right people do not meet the right other people at the right time the secret of baking the bread may be lost. Because it is not enough to eat the bread. You have to meet the woman who knows how to make it."

Her inner search continued. She went on looking for *the* way, *her* way. Was it to be through books? As an artist? And still she was concerned with the fact that people themselves were treasure chests of precious information about human life, some of which information, for instance, existed only among primitive people, in their living presence, for they did not read or write.

Again a book revealed to her how deeply she felt about the possible loss of human "ships" that might not be brought ashore. The book was *The Mystery of Easter Island* by a Mrs. Scoresby Routledge, who had travelled by ship and had searched for many weeks for the tiny little island known mostly by rumor for its strange huge statues that had undecipherable writing on the backs of them. When Mrs. Routledge finally arrived at Easter Island, the last man there who, it was believed, could interpret the legends on the statues, was too ill to tell his story. He died two weeks later and his valuable secrets died with him. Again Margaret felt the impact of the terrible fragility of human tradition—here again, the single human being and a ship that arrived too late.

Chapter 4

College and Commitment

World War I was over. Most of the young men had come home. College was to mean gaiety and dancing—the word "dating" was just coming into use. In the spring of 1919 after Margaret had been struggling to learn three years of French in one at the school in New Hope, Margaret's mother and father began talking about college plans for her. Since Margaret's mother had attended Wellesley, it had almost been taken for granted that Margaret would go there too. But now Margaret's father began to raise questions about whether this was such a good idea. He inspected the Wellesley catalogue and objected to the same old women teachers who had been there in her mother's day. He even raised questions as to what use there was in educating a girl who was just going to get married anyway.

Then the family doctor pronounced Margaret too frail to stand college work and suggested she be trained as a nurse instead. He pointed to her hands with their tiny nails—too small for half-moons to show—and said: "Look at those useless little hands. Never did a day's work in their life and never will." And he pronounced against college and for nursing—obviously not making any sense at all. Margaret recalls that she felt her only really violent attack of feminism. "I was actually going to school, taking three years of French in one, two courses in English, one in Bible, and one in trigonometry, keeping house for seven people, and preparing to play Jacques in *As You Like It* at the same time."

Years afterwards Margaret's father admitted that his real objection to her going to college had been financial. He had business ventures that weren't turning out well and that he didn't want to discuss with her mother. But her mother, unaware of this, chose a new strategy. She gave up the idea of Margaret's going to Wellesley and suggested she go instead to De Pauw University in Greencastle, Indiana, which had been her father's college. This idea appealed to Margaret's father. The tuition there was much less. He liked the idea of her being taught by one of his old classmates, and becoming, of course, a Theta, which he remembered as the ranking sorority of his day. And then and there he changed his mind about Margaret *not* going to college.

Delighted to get to college on any terms, Margaret was enthusiastic at the idea of going to the Midwest. She had been raised on all sorts of glowing mythology about Adams County in Ohio where her grandmother had spent her childhood, and about Chicago—the magical city where every child had a microscope, and where her mother had gone to high school and done amazing things like having a friend who became an explorer in Tibet. Since, therefore, such places as Adams County and Chicago were, by report, so magnificent, and everyone there (so it was said) was quite superior and democratic, it seemed logical that De Pauw would be exciting too. She gave up the thought of going to Wellesley with no particular qualms and began to pack for De Pauw.

Into her luggage went a tea set, photographs for the walls of her room, including a portrait of the Indian poet, Rabindranath Tagore, and her clothes, "compounds of an artist turned designer in New Hope and my own fancies faithfully executed by our visiting seamstress," which turned out to be "appallingly out of step with undergraduate styles in Indiana."

Margaret arrived on campus quite innocent of what she would find. She had never heard of rushing or of all the rules and restrictions that regulate the competition among sororities and fraternities. When she went to the Kappa party, "My aunt's friend took one look at my dress [it was one of her highly individual creations] and cut me dead. None of the women who had been my father's classmates were allowed by Panhellenic rules to speak to me. For the first, and last, time in my life I learned what it was to be a member of an outgroup, of a disapproved and disregarded minority. Everything about me was wrong—my accent, my taste, my clothes, my room, my past schooling." Forced to find things that a girl who had not made a sorority could do, Margaret wrote the dormitory stunt for Homecoming Week, wrote the college pageant, planned a political campaign that elected the first non-sorority vice-president of the student body. She also learned "how hateful it was to be a member of a minority group, because of the lack of loyalty that results among those who are such members. A minority position breeds an automatic lack of confidence and solidarity as each one hopes to escape into the majority. It is a lesson I might never have had a chance to learn." At the end of the year she persuaded her father to let her leave De Pauw and go to Barnard.

[49]

Barnard College in the upper part of New York City was, happily, nothing like De Pauw with its emphasis on sororities and football games and its lack of emphasis on anything like intellectual life. Barnard was a girl's college, but with Columbia University just across Broadway there were plenty of men and boys about. There were no sororities; they had been abolished a few years before. And to Margaret's great satisfaction the college was right in the center of New York. Subways and buses and taxis put the city's intellectual, artistic, and political life at her doorstep. Above all, at Barnard she found her own kind of people, friends with whom she could really share the things that excited her. "We talked endlessly about poetry, and the theatre, about Freud and Marx, about the new mathematics, about the settings of Robert Edmund Jones for *Macbeth*, about John Barrymore in *Hamlet*, about Eugene O'Neill and Pirandello, about the future of India, the fate of Sacco and Vanzetti, the future of the world. We were a group of very diverse students; socially we led such different lives that a couple of evening coats sufficed for all of us; but together, on the campus, we were able to form long and lasting friendships." One of her friends gave her a copy of Middleton Murry's *Shakespeare and Keats* and wrote a line from Callimachus on the fly leaf that to this day reminds her of her life on the Barnard and Columbia campus: "Where we tired the sun with talking."

Barnard and Columbia share a high hill on the west side of upper Manhattan, and many of Barnard's buildings, its dormitories and classrooms and tennis courts, border Riverside Drive. When Margaret was there, the big gray stone tower of Riverside Cathedral, which now dominates the campus, had not yet been built; but Grant's Tomb overlooking the Hudson was there, and so was the terrace on Morningside Heights and 116th Street from which one could look out over a huge spread of park and apartment buildings, and far off the smokestacks of factories and a gleam of the East River. Sometimes Margaret used to stand there early in the day and think of the lines of a Wordsworth sonnet:

> *This city now doth like a garment wear*
> *The beauty of the morning. . . .*

Margaret shared an apartment used as a dormitory at 606 West 116th Street with five other girls. The apartment had only five small rooms. Two girls slept in a bedroom, one in the dining room, one in the maid's room—which was very tiny and had a swinging door so that if someone was studying they could be pushed into it—and two girls slept in the living room. One of them was Margaret Mead.

Besides carrying a full schedule of classes, Margaret took part in many extracurricular activities: working on the college paper (in her senior year she became its editor), intercollegiate debating, organizing a political discussion supper club that met on Sunday night in the basement of the college chapel. She baby-sat before the word was invented as a way of getting long evenings for study, explored lectures at the New School for Social Research on relativity, taught Sunday school in Hell's Kitchen—"with dozens of small children hard to discipline under an unmovable pool table"—helped the social and political discussion club, served on the student committee for revising the curriculum, received general honors for a large accumulation of A's, tried to keep track of her two pairs of long white kid gloves (essential if one went dancing on Saturday afternoons), started doing graduate work as a senior. Margaret recalls: "They were crowded, delightful, intense years, full to the brim with excitement and achievement."

Of all her studies, classes in social sciences interested Margaret the most. In the early 1920's the social sciences were changing, developing, and for the first time taking a significant place in American life. The public was just beginning to see how important observations of sociologists might be for society—not only to understand such social ills as delinquency, alcoholism, and slums, but in the attempt to create better societies.

Because of her lifetime familiarity with the approach and methods of sociology, her mother's field, Margaret began to feel quite sure that her future work lay somewhere in this direction. Psychology, still quite new, and with its focus on the individual was fascinating to her. Then, in the fall semester of her senior year at Barnard, she enrolled in the class of Professor Franz Boas, a prime mover and pioneer in the field of anthropology, "father" of almost all American anthropologists, a German by birth, a dedicated pacifist, a profound humanist. He was, when Margaret first began attending his class, a professor who was then without a department, for anthropology had been kept down to a minimum. But in the very early weeks of the course, "anthropology began to come alive" for Margaret Mead. "Professor Boas with his great head and slight frail body, his face scarred from an old duel, and one eye dropping from a facial paralysis, spoke with an authority and a distinction greater than I had ever met in a teacher." His teaching became "the ground under my feet."

Having stumbled, in a sense, into anthropology, Margaret Mead recognized before long that this seemed to be what she had been seeking for so long. Then, too, she quickly realized that the odd assortment of talents and interests she had acquired all seemed somehow to fit—to belong—to the role of the anthropologist. Here her ability to remember nonsense would help her to learn primitive languages quickly, for the best way to do that was simply to remember all kinds of sounds that seem to have no meaning at first. Her childhood, with its many moves and changes, had taught her to adapt herself quickly to unfamiliar situations and ways of living, a prime requirement for the ethnologist—the anthropologist who studies different cultures, which was the kind of anthropologist that Margaret was interested in being—when he goes into the field to far off primitive places to do his work.

The shifting pattern of Margaret's childhood had helped to make her a highly flexible person. She was at home with all kinds of people and had learned from birth never to make judgments on the basis of race or creed or differences of manners or religion. It was also important to her that as an anthropologist she could contribute to the world as a woman. Margaret liked being a woman. In anthropology women were badly needed, for in primitive cultures no man would ever be allowed into the confidence of the women in the group. Only a woman would be able to talk to other women, to learn the intimate details of their lives, their customs, and habits. Above all, as an anthropologist she would be able to try to satisfy her inexhaustible curiosity about human beings and try to answer the big questions: Why do they do what they do? and Who are we—all of us?

Her enthusiasm grew. Each class with Professor Boas was an experience. He prepared each lecture as if he was to give it before a hundred of his professional colleagues. Students often took the same course with him several times, for it was always different. The second semester of her senior year at Barnard, Margaret began attending all the available anthropology courses. They were almost all taught by Professor Boas—theory, linguistics, biometrics—"in dreadful concentration and with no quarter given to beginners or to those with a defective background. In the biometrics course I remember him saying one day, 'I am embarrassed. Some of you do not know the calculus. I will teach you the calculus.' In the brief 20 minutes left of the hour he did!"

Most of the curriculum came under the heading of methods. Students studied human growth, language, art, mythology, or religion; but above all they were made aware of the need to test and evaluate through comparative studies or by doing fieldwork the assumptions that had given rise to all the theories. They learned in this way never to take the work of other scientists for granted. Above all, Professor Boas made his students conscious of "a vast panorama, a landscape with only tiny points of illumination" in which each small study that they made would help to fill in that landscape, help to build a structure. In his classroom Margaret and the others often felt as if many dark corners were being flooded with light, and many bits of human knowledge were being drawn together to make new meaning. But though he was every inch a scientist—and a great one—Professor Boas never ceased to be a human being concerned with other human beings. No fact was abstract to him—they were all real and alive, and so his words were living and strong.

At this time Margaret made one of the important friendships of her life. In the autumn of 1922 she met Ruth Benedict, who was then assisting Professor Boas and studying with him at the same time. She was already in her late thirties, 15 years older than Margaret, and had come to Columbia University at a difficult time in her life. After seven years of a childless marriage to a man who had become a well-known biochemist, her own search for something meaningful to do had also ended in the classroom of Dr. Boas who, recognizing her extraordinary mind and her deep interest in anthropology, managed with his customary disregard for administrative rules, to get graduate credit for her past work so that she could quickly obtain her doctoral degree.

When Margaret first met Ruth Benedict, she was as an assistant to Professor Boas taking Margaret's class to the American Museum of Natural History to illustrate materials on the course. Margaret became curious about "Mrs. Benedict" and set out to become acquainted with her "while most of the class fretted against her inarticulate shyness and her habit of always wearing the same dress and that not a very becoming one." But Margaret found that Ruth Benedict's "vivid delight in the details of Northwest coast art and of the Toda kinship system gave life to the clarity and order of Professor Boas' presentation of man's development through the ages."

Strong bonds formed between Margaret and this sensitive creative woman who was to become one of the outstanding anthropologists of the century. Despite the difference in their ages, the two women had many interests and loves in common. Anthropology was, of course, one of them. But so was poetry. Ruth Benedict wrote poems and had published some under the pseudonym Anne Singleton, and Margaret, of course, wrote verse continually. They became fast friends. They often discussed poetry, exchanged poems. Some of the poems they wrote were written one in response to the other. Edward Sapir, an outstanding anthropologist and poet with whom both Ruth Benedict and Margaret Mead were to remain professionally and poetically close in the years 1923-1925, was publishing prolifically. Sapir dedicated two poems, "Zuni" and "Signal" to Ruth Benedict and "Ariel" to Margaret.

Ariel
(To M. M.)

Of the heedless sun are you an Ariel,
Rising through cloud to a discovered blue,
The windy, rocking landmarks travel through
And clamber up a crazy pinnacle.
Be wild, oblivious, nor think how fell
One mocking angel and a frightened crew
Through all the sunny pools of air into
The dark and wondrous ritual of Hell.

For you have footing poised and in your breast
The interchange of breath, both quick and slow.
Reckless, be safe. The little wise feet know
Sun-way and cloud's and sudden earthen aim,
And steps of beauty quicken into flame
Wherein you burn up wholly in arrest.

Ruth Benedict wrote "This Gabriel" for Margaret:

He wrought a pitiful permanence
From jagged moments, and dismay,
And tears more purposeless than pain.
He smiled, knowing the gray

And dusty journey for the same
Men saw upwinding through the stars;
Himself no less infinity
Then they. He liked their common scars.

The better for their being won
As his upon a simple tree,
Wounding a transience and a flesh
Innocent of divinity.

What comfort had he had in praise
That makes of him this Gabriel
Walking the stars, his even pace
Shaped to a crystal citadel?

And Margaret wrote "Misericordia" for Ruth Benedict.

Summer, betray this tree again!
Bind her in winding sheets of green;
With empty promises unlock her lips;
Sift futile pollen through her finger-tips.
Curve those tense hands so tightened in disdain,
To eager chalices for falling rain.
Break and elaborate that frozen line
With golden tendril and swift sinuous vine.
Summer, in mercy blur this bare delight
Of chiseled boughs against this winter night.

For Ruth Benedict, Margaret Mead was many things—
sister, child, friend, colleague. Once Ruth wrote of Margaret in
her diary after she and Margaret had had a long talk: "She

rests me like a padded chair and a fireplace. I say it's the zest of youth I believe in when I see it in her."

To Margaret, Ruth Benedict, who had herself just found Professor Boas, was able to pass on many things which she herself had received from him. Among them were "a double feeling of urgency. The need to learn everything he had to teach, and to rescue the beautiful complex patterns that people had contrived for themselves to live in that were being irrevocably lost all over the world."

Many primitive cultures were disappearing rapidly with not enough trained anthropologists to record their ways of life before the onslaught of Western civilization—industrialization, transportation, missionary zeal—was to flatten out the striking differences of their cultures. This situation greatly intensified Margaret Mead's eagerness to become an anthropologist. Because these simpler societies were different enough to "startle and enlighten" the anthropologist, they were able to reveal much about our own complex societies by contrast, making it possible to see which qualities were in human beings simply because they are part of the human race as distinct from those qualities that people have learned from different complex patterns of life. But time was scarce. Each primitive society was being touched by "progress." Their people were being exploited commercially; they were losing their own religions. European diseases to which they had little resistance were being spread, and canned and overrefined Western foods were being introduced. The anthropologist was losing his only laboratories. For, unlike the chemist or the biologist, the anthropologist cannot study his subjects in a walled-in glass laboratory. He cannot point telescopes at them to watch them, or put them all together in a glass jar and observe them the way a biologist watches fruit flies. The anthropologist is dependent on these few fast disappearing, unsophisticated cultures (there are almost none left today) if he wants to observe how man lived under much simpler conditions. This sense of a need to make haste was never forgotten in the Columbia Department of Anthropology to which Margaret now belonged completely. When she received her B.A. from Barnard in 1923, she was certain of what she wanted to do, and she set about to find ways to support herself while taking higher degrees in anthropology. She worked as an editorial assistant on the *Journal of the American Statistical Association* and as a departmental assistant and secretary to sociology professor William F. Ogburn.

She found the atmosphere in the anthropology department at Columbia an exciting one, for in the early 1920's under the direction of such men as Franz Boas, Alfred Kroeber, Robert Lowie, and Clark Wissler, the young science had just begun to spread its wings. Just as a man who explores the continents of the earth or moves up into space in a rocket goes into the physical unknown, anthropologists were charting human unknowns, often taking risks as great as any aviator. The pioneers in anthropology were developing new theories and methods to try to understand how various cultures came to be, how they changed, and how they affected the people who lived in them. This is particularly why the emphasis in ethnology, the division of anthropology that concentrates on primitive cultures, was continually changing.

Before the 1920's most anthropologists had been concerned almost completely with describing the details of simple societies: their ceremonies, work habits, dress, crafts, language, utensils, and so forth. But at the time Margaret came into the field, many anthropologists were studying culture-change, the way, for instance, a particular style of making baskets developed among a people, or how the design on the border of a blanket came to be what it was. Some anthropologists were interested in diffusion—how a tribe or group acquired some cultural trait, perhaps a special dance or a manner of catching fish, through contact with another society. Others, such as Ruth Benedict and Edward Sapir, were beginning to show how "patterns of culture" could be distinguished within any given society.

But these studies were not, of course, confined to the offices and classrooms of the anthropology department—four small rooms on the seventh floor of the Journalism Building at 116th Street and Broadway. The far-off places where students and faculty went to do their fieldwork were just as real, and their comings and goings a routine part of the university's life. For fieldwork is the heart of an anthropologist's work, and anthropologists date events in the past as to whether they happened before, during, or after a field trip.

During these trips, anthropologists, especially if they are very close friends, as Margaret Mead and Ruth Benedict were, like to keep in touch. Ruth Benedict made many of her studies of the Zuni Indians and spent several summers there in Southwest New Mexico. In the summer of 1924 Margaret wrote to her, first from Holicong, Pennsylvania:

. . . I don't like to think of you all alone, though in many ways I suppose it will be less of a conversational strain at least. I wish we could go on a field trip together, only in my present state I'd talk you insane. I don't seem to be able to stop talking any more than I can stop thinking:

When I am dead, or sleeping
Without any pain,
My soul will stop creeping
Through my jewelled brain.

Only there I disagree with Elinor Wylie. At present I'm sure my soul won't ever stop. It's discovered perpetual motion in a circle. I have a few things I've written this summer which I will send you when I have time to type them. They are very bad, but I think it's important for you to see the worst things I'm capable of. You are too encouraging.

And a few weeks later, this, from New York City.

Be lazy, go crazy, be lazy, go crazy. I'll finish that charm off. This week when I had planned to accomplish so much I celebrated by getting a piece of glass in my eye and as a result got nothing done. It got in on the way to a conference with Goldy too, and finally arrived looking the picture of woe. . . .

Dr. Boas isn't returning till the end of the month and the world seems full of people who wander disconsolately until his return. . . . Your letter sounded about eight times too industrious. Aren't you really awfully tired out? Eleven hours of dictation makes me think of the day I gave thirteen Binets, and the memory is a most unsavory one.

Sending a student into the field for the first trip is always a major decision for a teacher. Professor Boas gave great thought to the problem a student was to work on, and the location where he or she could work best. By 1924 he was concerned with many new problems to be studied; he was interested for the first time in the role of the individual in a culture. In 1924 he sent Ruth Bunzel, a fellow graduate student of Margaret's, on a field trip to the Zuni Indians in the Southwest of the United

States to study the creative imagination and the place of the individual in art. Then in 1925 he suggested that Margaret Mead, who was feverishly anxious to set off on a project of her own—and who used to "wake up in the morning with the dreadful thought that the last man on Raratonga might be dying this very morning"—should go to study adolescence among a primitive people. But she was to do this with a very particular question in mind and for a very definite reason.

The question grew out of a problem and a controversy in the United States, where parents, teachers, sociologists, and psychologists had become increasingly concerned about the difficulties of the American adolescent. Many American psychologists described adolescence as the period "in which idealism flowered and rebellion against authority waxed strong," as Margaret later stated, and they concluded that adolescence was a period during which difficulties and conflicts were inevitable. The anthropologists however—or some of them—were aware from their own work with primitive peoples of how important a role the social environment in which an individual is born and reared plays in his life and in the forming of his personality. Thus the anthropologists were not at all sure that adolescent troubles were inevitable. Professor Boas questioned whether any attitude or habit—such as moodiness and tempers in adolescents—could be due just to being human; for almost everything discovered by anthropologists had proved that "humanity was infinitely malleable by society"—that is that human beings could be molded in many forms, almost like the clay that a sculptor or a potter can make into whatever shape he pleases.

Many years later, in *People and Places*, a book that Margaret wrote for children, she explained this idea in the following way: that any child could be reared from birth, or from a very early age, to think and believe and act in many different ways depending upon how and what he or she was taught. A Chinese baby brought up in the United States would still look, when he was grown, Chinese, but his way of thinking and acting would be American. And an Eskimo baby brought up in France would become an adult who, of course, spoke French and would have little interest in igloos or in hunting seals. And as for "just human nature," which so many people all over the world spoke of as if it really existed, there was no such thing. For while in some societies it was "human nature" to fight and be warlike; in others it was "human nature" to be peaceful and calm and loving. Now Boas wanted to know—could it possibly be "human nature" for all young adults between the ages of, say, 13 to 18, to be stormy and difficult?

The question had been raised. Were the so-called "inevitable" problems of adolescence "due to being adolescent or to being adolescent in America?" If one society existed where the pangs associated with adolescence in America did not occur, the question would be answered. Professor Boas hoped that Margaret would choose to make her observations of some group in or near the United States. She was very young—only 23— she was frail and thin, and her health was not perfect. But Margaret, whose doctoral thesis had been titled "The Relative Stability of Different Elements of Culture in Polynesia," had her heart set on going to Polynesia. But if it was to be Polynesia, Professor Boas insisted that it must not be too remote an island. So Samoa was chosen.

Samoa was, in fact, an ideal place to try to answer the question about adolescents. Although Samoa had been under

American control since 1899, it had, by some miracle remained as close to a natural paradise as any place on the globe —its people were fundamentally unspoiled.

In the case of Samoa, contact with European civilization had not destroyed genuine Samoan culture but had made life a bit more comfortable and in some ways less brutal than it had been in earlier times. Such violent practices as cannibalism, tribal warfare, blood revenge, and the life and death power of heads of households were now forbidden. Medical knowledge had helped cut down the enormous loss of life because of disease. Missionaries had introduced the concept of the mercy of God without much emphasis on the doctrine of original sin and damnation, and they had allowed the people to keep to the simplicity of their own ways. The American Naval government rarely interfered in native matters. The schools taught little more than reading and writing, elementary hygiene, and a few sports. The English language was not required, and few natives spoke it. European products, such as scissors, china, glassware, and knives, were occasionally used; but Samoans still dug their gardens with a sharpened pole, fished from the sea with nets and hooks made by Samoan men, the women still wove their own mats. The native arts had not been lost.

And so Samoa remained an ideal laboratory for Margaret Mead to make her new kind of research. It was one that was in many ways quite new and for which there were no blueprints.

That summer of 1925 before setting off for Samoa, Margaret spent on the farm in Holicong, Pennsylvania, mostly preparing for her first field trip. Her colleagues and teachers, however, who were scattered about the country, could not help being concerned about her health, though actually Margaret suffered from little more than neuritis—mostly in her arms.

On July 16, 1925, Professor Boas at Columbia University wrote Ruth Benedict this letter:

My dear Ruth,

Sapir had a long talk with me about Margaret Mead. You know that I myself am not very much pleased with this idea of her going to the tropics for a long stay. It seems to my mind, however, and it has seemed to my mind ever since I prevented her going to the Tuamotu [remote islands in the South Seas], that it would be much worse to put obstacles in her way that prevented her from doing a piece of work on which she had set her heart, than to let her run a certain amount of risk. . . . Of course I know that Margaret is high strung and emotional, but I also believe that nothing would depress her more than inability on account of her physical make-up and her mental characteristics to do the work she wants to do. In my opinion an attempt to compel her now to give up the trip . . . would be disastrous. Besides, it is entirely against my point of view to interfere in such a radical way with the future of a person for his or her own sake. . . . I should like to hear from you, if possible, at once."

And on July 18th, Ruth Benedict answered him.

Dear Dr. Boas,

. . . I agree heartily with your position in regard to Margaret. . . . Last spring I sent her to two doctors of the highest standing . . . and they could find nothing organically wrong. The diagnosis is nervous fatigue and they prescribe rest. It seems to me that it is perfectly possible

that the natural relaxation of a tropical climate . . .
may be the best possible change for her. . . . I know
that a letter from you emphasizing the duty of care and
avoidance of risks would count very much with Margaret. . . .

But Dr. Boas had already written to Margaret as follows:

My dear Margaret,

I suppose the time is drawing near when you want to
leave. Let me impress upon you once more, first of all,
that you should not forget your health. I am sure you will
be careful in the tropics and . . . not work when it is too
hot and moist in the daytime. If you find you cannot stand
the climate do not be ashamed to come back. There are
plenty of other places where you could solve the problem
on which you propose to work.

One question that interests me very much is how the
young girls react to the restraints of custom. We find very
much among ourselves during the period of adolescence a
strong rebellious spirit that may be expressed in sullen-
ness or in sudden outbursts. In other individuals there is
a weak submission which is accompanied, however, by a
suppressed rebellion that may make itself felt in peculiar
ways, perhaps in a desire for solitude which is really an
expression of desire for freedom, or otherwise in forced
participation in social affairs in order to drown the mental
troubles. I am not at all clear in my mind in how far similar conditions may occur in primitive society and in how
far the desire for independence may be simply due to our
modern conditions and to a more strongly developed in-
dividualism.

. . . Another interesting problem is that of crushes among girls. For the older ones you might give special attention to the occurrence of romantic love, which is not by any means absent as far as I have been able to observe, and which, of course, appears most strongly where the parents or society impose marriages which the girls may not want.

. . . Stick to individual and pattern, problems like Ruth Bunzel on art in Pueblos and Haeberlin on Northwest coast. . . . Good luck. I hope you will let me know soon how you are getting on. I trust that your trip will be successful in every way. Don't forget your health.

With kindest regards,

But Margaret was about to go very far from such advice and precious direction. In mid-August she boarded the train for San Francisco. There she embarked on the S. S. *Matsonia* for Honolulu. One of the last letters she received before sailing was this one from Ruth Benedict.

. . . This mail is the last that will surely catch the boat from San Francisco. I know I can't make all the beauty you'll be surrounded by, anything but aching pains. . . . And other times you must just love it because you are you and indomitable in the long run. After all, this is the only safety in life . . . and we always fight through to it in agony of soul. There is nothing else that is truly safe to build on, and we lay the miserable foundation over and over again. There is only one comfort that comes out of it—unbelievably—the sense that there is that sure something within us, no matter how often it is laid in ruins, that cannot be taken away from us.

Chapter 5

Makelita Goes to School

"May you most honorable enter," said Chief Ufuti.

"I have humbly come saving the presence of your Lordship and her who sits in the back of the house," answered Margaret.

"Alas for the coming of your Ladyship," said Chief Ufuti, "there is nothing good in the house."

"Oh let the matter rest," replied Margaret correctly. "It is of no consequence whatsoever."

And so indeed it had all begun—a new stage in Margaret's education as an ethnologist, with new teachers quite quite different from those at Columbia—in the Village of the Turtle and the Shark.

She liked Chief Ufuti from the first moment.

"His voice," she recalls, "was soft and kind, his eyes clear, penetrating and gentle, his face had the delicacy and breeding of an old line of nobility. His wife, Sava, whom I was to learn to call 'mother' was plump and every dimple in her face held an extra bit of kindliness and good humor. Then there was the Chief's daughter, Fa'amotu, his two sons, a small girl named Tulip, and a baby boy."

The first evening Margaret spent in a Samoan village there was another ceremony; for she had been told she was not, like other visitors, to stay in the guest house but that she would share a bed with Fa'amotu.

Making the bed turned out to be a matter of great formality in which Sava, Fa'amotu, and several other Samoan girls took part. First, the floor of the house, which like most Samoan houses was made of small gray pieces of coral and always swept immaculately clean with a short, whisk-like broom, was spread carefully with the heavy, coarse mats that the women brought down from the rafters where they were kept stored all day along with all the other "furniture"—chairs, tables, all were made of mats. Each mat takes a Samoan woman a full month of steady work to plait. Now Margaret watched the women pile one mat upon another, telling, as they did this, the story of each mat and where it came from—one from Savai'i, another from Tokelau, and so forth. Soon the bed was several inches off the ground. Then a snow-white mosquito net was hung from the rafters straight to the floor, where it was weighted round the edge with stones. Next, two hard white pillows were placed at the head of the bed, and then a spotlessly clean white sheet was spread over it.

That night Margaret found that "a mat bed was quite cool and comfortable if you lay on your back," and that the mosquito net kept her safe not only from flies and mosquitoes but also from the dogs and little pigs and casual chickens that sometimes wandered into the house. She also noticed, with a small shock, that her bedroom had only one wall to divide her from the rest of the family, but that the other three sides were totally open to the eyes of the villagers. She came to understand later the Samoans do not feel it is necessary to erect walls between people. They simply look away from each other at times. It was only, she realized, "because I was white and a stranger, and they knew white people had funny ideas, that they had hung up the curtain."

Waking that first morning in the Village of the Turtle and the Shark was an experience Margaret was never to forget. "Down on the sea edge could be heard the violent splash of the surf against the dark lava coast . . . and great jets of white spray could just be glimpsed through the pale light. The Samoans on rising wrap themselves in their sheets and go down to the beach for the morning toilet, and here and there white robed figures followed by tiny naked ones were moving slowly, still tranced in sleep, down to the sea. From the little cooking houses slow spirals of smoke rose lazily, disappearing among the palm leaves which were catching the first rays of the rising sun. A muted sound of low greetings and low exhortations to children fluttered through the village. And Fa'amotu sat up in bed and whispered, 'Makelita' "—for this was the way of saying her Samoan name—". . . it is morning."

Living with Chief Ufuti and his family, Margaret was not only able to practice the language everyday, but she soon began to accustom herself to totally new habits—she learned to sit cross-legged on the ground, never to speak when standing, to eat with her fingers from a woven plate. And when Chief Ufuti realized that Makelita, who soon became used to the sound of her name, was not like the other foreign visitors that came only to look and then leave but that she really meant to spend many moons in Samoa, and was sincerely anxious to learn all she could about "Samoan politeness," he asked the talking chief Lolo to become her teacher in this crucially important sphere. Margaret knew perfectly well that without understanding and observing the highly developed rules of Samoan courtesy, she would never be able to be fully accepted by all the various levels of Samoan society, and she applied herself to this new undertaking with zest and concentration.

The kava ceremony was perhaps the most important of all Samoan rituals. The talking chief Lolo, a jolly man who laughed at her mistakes but could also become stern unless she corrected them at once, began to teach Makelita how to pass the coconut cup that held the sharp astringent drink called kava, which Samoans drink at every major event. Makelita learned, she recalls,—"how I must place my left hand, palm out against the small of my back and raise my right hand in which the handleless shell of liquid was carefully cupped, high above my head, then sweep it slowly to the ground—*if* I was serving a chief. For a talking chief I had to make a different and simpler gesture." After Makelita had performed these gestures several times, Lolo announced that she would serve the kava to the chiefs that same afternoon. Margaret was horror-stricken, for she knew that if an insect or a piece of windblown down were to fall into the great carved bowl in which the kava was made, the Samoans believed a terrible misfortune would befall the village. More terrifying, she knew that each chief had his own kava cup—and that each kava cup had its own flowery name. How, she wondered, when the talking chief called out the name of the cup, would she know which chief the cup was to go to. But Lolo saved face for Makelita—when a chief's cup was called, he clapped his hands gently to indicate which one she was to serve. Miraculously the ceremony went smoothly.

She learned to dance, too, for in Samoa everyone dances from chiefs to the smallest shiest children. A *taupo*, a Samoan princess, must learn to dance in a grave, aloof, beautiful manner; and since Makelita was being taught the etiquette used by Samoan royalty, she too learned for the most part to dance this way. But Makelita never forgot that each new acquired skill or understanding or capacity for living in the Samoan way was to help Margaret Mead as anthropologist do the job for which she had come, and that only when she felt fully immersed in this gentle South Sea island culture would she be able to see the real social underpinnings of which it was made. But she was grateful that, in this, her first experience as a working ethnologist in the field, she was among this dignified and friendly people. She felt in many ways deeply "at home," and the strange adventure of shedding her own way of life and adopting a new one was not quite as strange as it might have been.

There was still more for Margaret to learn of Samoan formality. And then, one day, Lolo felt Makelita was ready for her final examination. He invited all the most important men of the Village of the Turtle and the Shark to come and hear his protégée speak. They came. They sat about very solemn, cross-legged, each one against a different post, and they began to ask Makelita questions to test her skill. It was difficult. "Far harder," she remembers, "than the doctoral examination I had had to pass at Columbia. I had to sit cross-legged with a perfectly straight back and arms folded, no matter how many flies flew trustfully under my chin, which is what Samoan flies like to do best. I must not move a finger to brush them away. And I had to juggle the proper verbs and nouns depending upon whether a man was a chief or a talking chief."

At the end came the worst question of all. A very old chief leaned forward and asked: "Why is it that you have elected to spend only two weeks here in this village and plan, so it is said, to go to the faraway island of Manu'a and spend six months?" The atmosphere was very tense. Then Margaret answered with all the tact and imagination she could summon. "If it please your lordship, when I planned to go to Manu'a I had not yet seen the Village of the Turtle and the Shark." There was a great sigh of relief in the open room, and one man murmured to the others, "The proper courtesy answer." And Makelita was saved. For, as she had come to know, Samoans cared most of all for the manner in which a thing is said.

But graduation from Professor Lolo and the house of Chief Ufuti meant it was time to leave "her family," and that they had truly become to her a family to whom she knew she could go and say, " 'I'm poor, I'm sick'—and they would have taken care of me. They were my people." She put her baggage—the metal cashbox, the photos, the poetry book, what she had of clothing, and, of course, the little pillow—on a Navy minesweeper, and left for the island of Tau, a journey of only a few hours.

The island of Tau was guarded by a great coral reef that made it perilous for any ship, even the Navy minesweeper, to approach the island. The reef was an ever present reality of life on Tau. Because of the reef it was never sure whether or not mail would arrive, or food from Pago Pago, or if a group of returning chiefs would set foot on the beach in dry regalia or struggle through the waves pushing their canoe before them. Every vessel had to find the small opening in the reef and then ride over the waves at just the right moment—or else the boat was sure to overturn. At just the instant the Navy boat that Margaret was on made it through the reef, another boat, less fortunate, overturned, spilling scores of Samoan schoolchildren into the water. It was a frightening moment till Margaret saw that the children were all marvelously schooled in reef-swimming, and there would be no tragedies.

On Tau, it had been arranged by the Naval authorities in Pago Pago that Margaret was to stay with Mr. Edward R. Holt, Chief Pharmacist Mate on the island, his wife Ruth, and their two small children, Arthur and the new baby, Moana. The Holt house was more or less a European type of construction. It had several rooms. There was a clinic, living room and dining room, a radio room, the babies' room, and there were two porches—a front porch and a back porch. Margaret slept on the back porch, which was closed in by one wall and one lattice work screen; but the rest was quite exposed to public view and in this respect truly Samoan. Villagers, especially the girls who were Margaret's companions and subject matter for her study, often came by to peek at Makelita and see if she was still asleep. There was little privacy, but then Margaret knew by now that Samoans believed no one ever sought solitude unless it was to do or think some evil thing.

Though Margaret might have preferred in some ways to live in a Samoan house and with a Samoan family, it was good to be able to sit on a chair and type at a table instead of on the floor, and it was good to have some light to type by. Occasionally she was glad for the extra comforts and conveniences, though these were of minimum importance to her. Every so often she was grateful for the chance to speak English. And, as she was to write later in her book, *Coming of Age in Samoa*, the Holt's home furnished her "with an absolutely essential neutral base from which I could study all the individuals in the village and yet remain aloof from native feuds and lines of demarcation."

Nevertheless, there were times when she felt overprotected. Particularly when the minister on Samoa sent one of his girls to be her constant companion. And when she felt herself

caught between the subtle pulls of two sets of status systems—
the Samoan and that of the American Navy. "I had to worry
about both," she remembers. "I couldn't avoid it." The Samoans felt she was a high status visitor; when she went visiting she
was treated as a *taupo*, a Samoan princess; they did not, however, understand her desire to spend most of her time with the
children. But it was only from the children that Margaret could
get the information she had come for. So she decided that by
playing the role of what would be more or less a school teacher,
she could avoid the local confusion, satisfy the minister, the
Samoan chiefs, the Navy officials, and the adolescent girls she
had come to study—without offending anyone.

On New Year's Day, only a month after Margaret's arrival on Tau, a severe hurricane struck the island and destroyed
almost all the village. Instead of being afraid, Margaret was
curious to see how the Samoan men protected themselves, their
families, and their homes from the big winds. But Mr. Holt and
the other men considered Margaret at that moment not as a
scientist but simply as another American woman to be protected—and she found herself placed inside a big empty tank
that stood behind the house. She was hoisted up on a ladder and
lifted over the tank's eight-foot wall. Then she stood on a high
box inside the tank and they handed her the Holt's little boy
Arthur, and then the baby in a wash basin that had to serve as
a cradle. Then they left her alone, listening to the raging winds
and the waves. It seemed hours before the rest climbed in. Had
the winds changed at the peak of the storm, a tidal wave might
have swept over the entire island, and the tank could have protected them.

When the hurricane was over, the villagers began to re-
build their devastated homes. Margaret was quickly becoming
accepted as almost a Samoan girl since she made every effort to

learn to do many of the tasks Samoan girls were expected to do: to gather bananas, taro, breadfruit; select leaves to use for cooking; cut coconuts to make copra; skin the bananas and grate the coconut in order to mix palusami, a pudding made from coconut and flavored with a red hot stone; pound the kava root and make the kava. She watched how the Samoan girls made bark cloth by gathering paper mulberry wands, then scraping the bark, then pounding the bark, and how they used a pattern board or traced the patterns freehand. In the house a Samoan girl's principal task was to learn to weave, mastering several different techniques—making carrying baskets from palm branches, or the Venetian blinds that hang between the houseposts by laying one half leaf upon another and plaiting the leaflets together—or weaving the floor mats, which are much more difficult, from the pandanus, a special leaf that when soaked and baked and scraped to a golden whiteness and paperlike thinness can be woven into a mat soft and pliable as linen and greatly valued among the Samoans. But these last take a year or two years to make, and Makelita did not have that much time.

In Samoa the pattern of life was simple and clear. As girls and boys reached adolescence they were not made to feel that they had to make any crucial or painful choices or decisions, ones that might divorce them from family or group loyalties; for in Samoa there was only *one* fundamental set of beliefs and conduct, and everyone took part in it. And since in Samoa many adults filled the role of father or mother for a child (many women were called "mother" and many men "father"), no girl or boy felt trapped or dependent upon any one person for affection or approval. She, or he, knew one could always move across the street to some other relative. Margaret saw too how the Samoan children were not only allowed but were expected to see everything that happened around them. Before they were very old they were no strangers to death, birth, funerals, pregnancies; and since courtship and lovemaking took place so much in the open, they were familiar with those natural practices too. It seemed to Margaret that this open attitude to life protected the Samoan children in a real way from later feelings of shock, repulsion, horror, and fear that so often afflicted American children.

And in the Samoan attitude towards work for their children, Margaret observed how even little children learned responsibility and to be a part of the adult world in a natural, simple way. For girls of four or five were expected to take care of their smaller brothers and sisters to help free their older sisters and their mothers to do the harder chores. And, as distinct from training in the United States and much of Europe, Samoan children did not learn to do adult things by playing with toys. Once she had a box of white clay pipes for blowing soap bubbles sent to her and tried to interest some Samoan children in playing with them. "But after a few minutes' delight in the unusual size and beauty of the soap bubbles, one little girl after another asked me if she might please take her pipe home to her mother, for pipes were meant to smoke not to play with. Foreign dolls did not interest them, and they had no dolls of their own. . . . They never make toy houses, nor play house, nor sail toy boats. Little boys would climb into a real outrigger canoe and practise paddling it within the safety of the lagoon." In this way the play of Samoan children, thought Margaret, had a dignity that the play of American children lacked.

Each day the things Margaret noticed about her helped to answer the questions she had come with. Night after night she pondered the differences she discovered between the two cultures—her own and that of Samoa. Sometimes it was hard to think clearly with the constant pounding of the waves on the reef, the torrid heat, the mosquitoes, the noise of the myna bird outside, the Holt's too present cat. The lack of privacy was at times annoying. And occasionally she was lonely for someone she could talk to about the things that really interested her. Boat day once every six weeks helped. The minesweeper that came from Pago Pago brought fresh meat, but it had to be cooked at once because there were no freezers. The boat brought film that had to be exposed immediately and shipped back on the same ship, or else the film would be destroyed by the intense heat and humidity. But the minesweeper also brought mail. Sometimes Margaret would receive 80 or 90 letters from the United States at one time. An avalanche! She would take them all back to her porch, spread them out on her bed and look at them, trying to imagine what news they might have to tell before she opened them.

Ruth Benedict was a steady correspondent. Once, soon after Margaret arrived, she sent this from Zuni:

> . . . This is the last morning in Zuni. . . . Yesterday we went up under the sacred mesa along stunning trails where the great wall towers above you always in new magnificence. . . . When I'm God I'm going to build my city there.

And a little later, from Santa Fe:

> I am glad you know how much of me is shut into your book of verses. I shall delight in having you feel me speaking them to you. Will you do one thing?—jot down the

verses you wish you had or the ones that haunt you brokenly, and I'll send them to you. . . . I wonder, is Samoa seething activity for you or peaceable? Do you find time or mood for verses? I hope so. . . .

Margaret herself was not always the best correspondent. Like most young people, when she was happy or busy she didn't bother to write. It was when things were difficult that she did. But she sometimes wrote long letters—to Professor Boas or Ruth Benedict or other colleagues—which she never mailed, when she reached a problem in her work that she did not understand, or where she felt she could have used "consultation" with a more experienced anthropologist. By thinking the problem out on paper, she discovered she could often make her way out of her confusion by herself.

When she had spent almost nine months on the islands of Samoa, Margaret felt that the work she had come to do was about finished. Besides she had received an exciting cable from the American Museum of Natural History in New York City confirming her appointment as assistant curator of ethnology, a most impressive position for a woman of Margaret Mead's young years. She was 24 years old. It was certainly time to return.

She packed her notes, all kinds of Samoan curios photographs, memories, impressions, ideas, and sailed for home. But this time she sailed backwards. First to Australia (there was a dreadful hurricane enroute), then into the Indian Ocean, up into the Red Sea, and at last through the Suez Canal into the blue peaceful Mediterranean to land at Marseilles, a port in the South of France.

She spent the summer in Europe—"a wonderful summer, for everyone in the world was there the summer of 1926," she recalls. She met her college roommate in Paris; later she went on to Rome to attend the Congress of Americanists, ethnologists and archaeologists from all over Europe. In early fall she left from a French port on the North Sea to finish her round-the-world trip, for that is what it had become. A few weeks later, Margaret Mead, who had embarked alone the year before from San Francisco arrived in New York harbor to be met by throngs of friends, relatives, teachers, and family. It was a very happy day.

Chapter 6

Margaret Mead Writes a Book

The American Museum of Natural History in New York City today is a long stone building facing Central Park on Manhattan's West Side, several city blocks long. The Museum's main entrance is inside a huge columned archway. To reach it one must go up a long flight of steps and past a large bronze statue of former President Theodore Roosevelt, who sits proudly on an enormous muscular steed. Both the horse and the President look unflinchingly ahead of them, and they are flanked, on one side by a tall Indian chief in a feathered headdress and on the other by a big bareheaded, bare-chested Negro. When the weather is good there are always sure to be a host of pigeons sitting happily on top of the famous Roughrider's head, on the horse's tail and mane, on the Indian's feathers.

Neither the statue, nor the archway, nor the Planetarium building were there in 1924 when Margaret Mead came back from Samoa and went right to work in the Museum as assistant curator of ethnology. She had been put in charge of all the exhibits and materials that had to do with Oceania—of which, of course, the Samoan islands were a part. Dr. Pliny Earl Goddard, Curator of Anthropology, had offered Margaret this job even before she went to Samoa, not only because she had already proved herself to be a capable and responsible anthropologist, but also because he sensed that she might have the flair for dramatic writing, the understanding of popular tastes and ways of thinking, and the lack of scientific snobbery that would make her just the right person to interpret the new science of anthropology to the American public.

And so, shortly after her return, Margaret Mead began to turn in every day at the entrance to the mammoth building at the corner of 78th Street and Columbus Avenue—an entrance that is now closed. Once inside the door she had to walk through the Plains Indians Hall and a large foyer filled with meteors, then take an elevator to the fifth floor, and then walk down a long, long corridor past row upon row of glass cases in which were stored all kinds of primitive sculptures and plates and bowls and weapons and costumes and jewelry and other artifacts. At the end of this seemingly endless hall, there was a short steep staircase on the right side that Margaret Mead had to climb; at the top of the stairs she had to make two or three more little turns past shelves and metal doors and rooms; and at last, hidden away so carefully that no one could find it without a guide, set into the roof of the Museum was Margaret Mead's office.

This very special office had been given to Margaret Mead because there was no other working space available on the main floor, and also because she was the youngest member of the department. (It had once been the living quarters of the chief engineer of the Museum because it was close to the lights and the switches and all the mechanical equipment.) But Margaret was delighted with her garret. She recalls, "I had always chosen the room at the top of every house we lived in. Here I had it!" When she first walked into the big square room with its three large windows looking out onto the long runway of the Museum's green-gabled roof and beyond to a jagged skyline of apartment buildings, there was nothing at all in the way of furniture except a big rolltop desk, a big table, a bookcase, and a few empty, low metal cupboards. There was room, though, lots of it, for Margaret to put a Samoan tapa, or bark cloth, and a map of the world up on the wall, to lay Samoan mats on the wooden floor, and to make curtains for the windows out of muslin stamped in tapa patterns by the Samoans.

The Museum guards were a bit bewildered at first. When Margaret taught her first class at the Museum and told a guard that she was "Dr. Mead," he said to her: "As if we didn't have trouble enough without making girls doctors." Another time she had similar trouble convincing a group of summer school students Ruth Benedict had sent down to the Museum so that "Dr. Mead" might show them something from "her hall" about "her people." Margaret was to take them to the Hall of Man first, and there she discovered that none of the students accepted a word she said to them. They had all read different books; all the dates were uncertain (this was before Carbon 14 dating had been developed); they all had their own ideas. They kept challenging Margaret, who didn't look any older than anyone in the group, until she finally lost her temper. She marched them up to the South Sea Hall, said it was "her hall," gave them a very rapid lecture using a lot of Polynesian words, and then, and only then, they seemed to realize this *was* Dr. Mead.

From that time on Margaret Mead's title and role went unchallenged, and she plunged into the enormous amount of work that lay ahead of her with intensity and enthusiasm. In the fall of 1926 she began to write her first book, the one that was to tell of what she had learned in Samoa about the problems of adolescence. With the help of notebooks, photographs, vivid memories, and many ideas all beginning to take form in her head, she set to work. (Not only did she want to describe the life of the Samoan girl—how she grew up, what she was taught to think, how she learned to act, the tasks she was expected to master, the manner in which she was courted, and so on—and to make scientific observations about how the Samoan girl's way of life differed from that of the American girl; but she also hoped to give the reader a sense of what Samoa was really like. So she began the first chapter:

The life of the day begins at dawn, or if the moon has shown until daylight, the shouts of the young men may be heard before dawn from the hillside. Uneasy in the night, populous with ghosts, they shout lustily to one another as they hasten with their work. As the dawn begins to fall among the soft brown roofs and the slender palm trees stand out against a colourless, gleaming sea, lovers slip home from trysts beneath the palm trees or in the shadow of beached canoes, that the light may find each sleeper in his appointed place. Cocks crow, negligently, and a shrill-voiced bird cries from the breadfruit trees. The insistent roar of the reef seems muted to an undertone for the sounds of a waking village. Babies cry, a few short wails before sleepy mothers give them the breast. Restless little children roll out of their sheets and wander drowsily down to the beach to freshen their faces in the sea. Boys, bent upon an early fishing, start collecting their tackle and go to rouse their more laggard companions. Fires are lit, here and there, the white smoke hardly visible against the paleness of the dawn. The whole village, sheeted and frowsy, stirs, rubs its eyes, and stumbles towards the beach.

The book was published in the summer of 1928. Before many months had gone by, it received all kind of critical attention. Reviewers, some of them of world renown, were almost unanimously delighted and impressed.

Nat J. Ferber, of the New York *American* wrote: "The author has made an astonishing study of the life of the Samoan girl . . . begins her work with a description of Samoa that is more beautiful than any I have ever read of this corner of the world."

The New York *Times* said the book had ". . . invaluable material against which to study better the conditions and problems of our own youth. . . . Her book, broad in its canvas and keen in its detail, is sympathetic throughout, warmly human, yet never sentimental, frank with the clean clear frankness of the scientist, unbiased in its judgment, richly readable in its style. It is a remarkable contribution to our knowledge of humanity."

In *Living Age*, the reviewer wrote: " . . . probably the most readable account of a remote civilization yet offered to the American public. . . . From her observations she fashions a startling commentary on our complex pattern of existence. She graces the scholarly soundness of her material with humor and lucidity of style."

George A. Dorsey of the New York *Herald Tribune* called the book ". . . an extraordinarily brilliant, and so far as I'm aware, unique piece of work."

The reviewer of the St. Louis *Daily Globe Democrat* said, "The picture of life and culture in Samoa is done so interestingly that romantic tales of the South Seas appear ordinary beside it—an endlessly fascinating history."

Havelock Ellis, author, philosopher, and himself a student of primitive peoples, wrote a letter to William Morrow, publishers of Margaret Mead's book, to say he thought it "Not only a fascinating book to read, but most constructive and valuable. Throughout one admires the sound judgement and fine insight of the author." Clarence Darrow, the famous attorney who defended the ideas of evolution in what came to be known as the Scopes Trial, or The Monkey Trial, called it "a very important book." And Dr. Bronislaw Malinowski, the eminent anthropologist whose own studies of South Sea Island peoples were widely read, called the book, "an absolutely first-rate piece of descriptive anthropology and an excellent sociological comparison of primitive and modern conditions. . . ."

There were few negative comments, but they were not without humor. Roger Sprague, reviewing the book in the *Saturday Review of Literature*, thought that Margaret had not really understood why the Samoan adolescents were free from conflict. He felt that it was simply because Samoans were closer to the "lower animals" and that the "hard productive toil of their lives" kept them too busy to be upset about anything; whereas, he wrote, ". . . certain it is that the New York girl, high or low, rarely has to work like a scrubwoman, and as Satan invariably finds some mischief still for idle hands to do, many observers have found her up to sufficient mischief." Still he thought Margaret had done "wonderfully well." A Mr. Nels Anderson wrote in *The Survey*, that he was undecided "whether it had been a contribution to science or art. If this is intended to be a work of art then the 'gay spirit,' and Dr. Mead's impressionistic style are in place. If it is science the book is somewhat of a disappointment. It lacks documental base. It is given too much to interpretation instead of description."

Such criticism did not faze Margaret at all. She knew precisely why she had written *Coming of Age in Samoa* in the colorful, easy-reading style she had; and years later in a preface she wrote for a new edition of the book she described her own book as "the first piece of work by a serious professional anthropologist written for the educated layman in which all the paraphernalia of scholarship designed to convince one's professional colleagues and confuse the laity was deliberately laid aside." As a scientist, she had no intention of letting anyone's "disappointment" that this book was not filled with scientific phraseology deter her from her longtime purpose. She wanted her books to reach a wide audience, and she wanted that audience not only to learn from what she had to tell them and to stimulate their thinking; but she wanted them to enjoy themselves at the same time. So she put her documentation into the appendix and into her scholarly monograph.

Before long Margaret's book became a best seller in many parts of the country and was a topic for discussion and debate. Parents, teachers, clergymen, sociologists, psychologists, anthropologists, all were fascinated by many of the contrasts between the life and education of the Samoan girl and that of the American adolescent. Margare Mead wrote that growing up in Samoa was easier than it was in the United States because of "the general casualness of the whole society. For Samoa is a place where no one plays for very high stakes, no one pays very heavy prices, no one suffers for his convictions or fights to the death for special ends"; while she thought that in the United States young people are forced to make too many difficult and crucial choices—choices of a job, of future work, of husband or wife, of political party, etc. She also wrote that young people were forced to make these choices too soon and without having been reared to be able to make *free* choices. American parents, she felt, too often imposed their own ideas on their children by exerting parental authority through the dispensing of money. As a result as soon as a girl or boy had an income of his or her own, "with no strings of morals or manners attached," parental authority usually falls. Most destructive were emotional pressures whereby young women and men were made to feel that should they choose to live by values or standards that are not those of their parents, they would lose their parents' love and approval. No Samoan parent, Margaret observed, would ever think of saying, "Be good to please mother," and she went on to say that "In our ideal picture of the freedom of the individual . . . it is not pleasant to realise that we have developed a form of family organisation which often cripples the emotional life, and warps and confuses the growth of many individuals' power to consciously live their own lives."

Still, when she asked this question of her readers: "What are the rewards of the tiny ingrown, biological family opposing its closed circle of affection to a forbidding world, of the strong ties between parents and children, ties which imply an active personal relation from birth until death?"—she had to admit that the high price "of many individuals' preserving through life the attitudes of dependent children" was paid "for the ability to feel and react as an individual in love and in marriage and in all human relationships"—an individuality and intensity of affection she had found lacking in Samoa— and therefore "a gain which we would not relinquish."

But Margaret Mead was searching for and believed there were answers and ways of training the young that ought to retain the gains of individuality made by Western civilization and yet reduce the conflicts of choice that were causing so much pain and waste to young Americans. In the last chapter of her book, called "Education for Choice," she went bravely on to venture some solutions or at least part-solutions, based on what she had learned in Samoa.

"We must," she wrote, "turn all of our educational efforts to training our children for the choices which will confront them. Education, in the home, even more than at school, instead of being a special pleading for one regime, a desperate attempt to form one particular habit of mind which will withstand all outside influences, must be a preparation for those very influences. . . . The child who is to choose wisely must be healthy in mind and body . . . and this child of the future must have an open mind. . . . The children must be taught how to think, not what to think. . . . They must be taught that many ways are open to them . . . and that upon them and upon them alone lies the burden of choice. Unhampered by prejudices . . . they must come clear-eyed to the choices which lie before them.

". . . we pay heavily for our heterogeneous, rapidly changing civilization; we pay in high proportions of crime and delinquency . . . in the conflicts of youth . . . in an ever-

[91]

increasing number of neuroses. . . . In such a list of prices we must count our gains carefully. . . . And chief among our gains must be reckoned this possibility of choice. . . ."

And she ended her book with a question put frankly to the American people.

"Samoa knows but one way of life, and teaches it to her children. Will we, who have the knowledge of many ways, leave our children free to choose among them?"

Mother, Father, Child

Emily Fogg Mead
as a university student

Edward Sherwood Mead
as a young professor

Margaret at four

Beginnings

Margaret Mead
at 16

Ruth Benedict

Professor Franz Boas

UNDERWOOD & UNDERWOOD

BLACKSTONE STUDIOS, NEW YORK

*Margaret Mead wearing
a wedding dress woven by
Makelita, last Queen of Manu'a*

With the youngest son of Chief Ufuti

New Guinea

*With Manus children
in the lagoon at Peri*

A Manus wedding

*Showing an Arapesh child
a brown American doll, 1932*

*Margaret Mead and
a Balinese baby, Karba, 1937*

*Karba with
a baby of his own, 1958*

The witch in the Balinese drama

Mother and Daughter

Cathy at 15 months

Cathy at four

Cathy at 10

LOTTE JACOBI

Before and After

With Manus children, 1928   *With a Manus' child grown up and his child, 1953*

Manus children listening to a tape recorder, 1953

*Talking over research
with Lawrence K. Frank*

*Catherine as a bride with
her father, Gregory Bateson*

*With Catherine and Barkev
at the Franks, Cloverly, N.H.*

*Catherine explains
work to her mother*

*Margaret Mead, Catherine, and Cloverly children
on White Oak Pond*

At Work

*Amidst preparations
for the Peoples
of the Pacific Hall
in the Museum*

KEN HEYMAN: MAGNUM PHOTOS

KEN HEYMAN: MAGNUM PHOTOS

Talking to students at International House, New York

Conferring in her office with an Indonesian student

Lecturing on closed-circuit television, 1960

Chapter 7

Dogs' Teeth, Ghosts, Spoiled Children in New Guinea

Margaret Mead wrote home from Lorengau, Manus, in the Admiralty Islands, Mandated Territory of New Guinea, on November 22, 1928: "This entrance into a new land of savages by way of the usual collection of ill-assorted white residents is as dull as usual. The steamer coming up the Marsina was a tiny evil-smelling little tub; but the menu boasted eighteen curries. . . . From Samarai we went to haul a stranded ship off a reef. Natives in flat wide canoes, bound together, floated about idly and at night built a fire in the center of the canoe, spread the sail over themselves as they lay in a circle, feet inwards. They were tied up to the ship's side and a whole hose of water was debouched over them by accident spreading disaster over the twenty sleepers. We pulled the *Morinda* off the reef, went to a concert on the *Montura* which was also standing by, climbed over the rail aboard the *Morinda* which had tied up alongside to refill her water tanks from our supply and maundered back to Samarai and so to Port Moresby. . . ."

And so began a new episode in Margaret Mead's life as an anthropologist. She was off to live with the Manus, some 2,000 dark-skinned, sea-dwelling people who lived off the coast of Manus, largest of the Admiralty Islands north of New Guinea. This was to be a new experience for Margaret Mead in other ways as well. This time she would work with her anthropologist husband, Reo Fortune. Not only would she now have someone to share the adventures and physical difficulties and to lessen the burden of loneliness, but as part of a husband and wife team in the field the work done could be, in many ways, more complete. As in almost all primitive tribes, the Manus men and women have sharply different roles and functions and secrets. Any single anthropologist can look at only one side of the total picture—as Margaret Mead had limited her study in Samoa to that of adolescent girls. But a man and woman working together are able to construct the story of an entire society from what they learn from both sexes.

Dr. Mead had, of course, her own special area of study in mind when they left for Manus. She was still concerned, as she had been in Samoa, with "the way in which each human infant is transformed into the finished adult": so it would be the Manus children on whom she would concentrate most of her attention. But in particular, she wanted to see whether animism (the belief that nonliving things such as stones possess the qualities of people—the way a child who hits the floor it has just fallen on believes the floor is wicked for hurting it) was present among the children of such primitive groups as the Manus. For in all the talking about animism Margaret Mead had noticed "no one had asked: 'If grown-up savages think like children, what do their children think like?'"

But as she left for this field trip she had little idea of what she might find among the Manus—far less than she had

had when she sailed for Samoa. The peoples of Manus had been less closely observed. She did know, however, that the Manus lived very much as they had for centuries. She knew that no missionaries had come to disturb the Manus' own complicated beliefs in ancestor worship. She knew that although they lived literally without land—on bits of volcanic rubble and a few man-made islands—or forests or gardens or fresh water, and had no wood to build their houses, the Manus were not, as one might imagine, the poorest people in the Admiralty Islands. The Manus were in fact the richest. Being expert fishermen and having constructed a fleet of fine canoes, they had become the most dominant trading people in the southern part of the archipelago. The inhabitants of the main island of the archipelago, known as the Usiai, depended on the fish and turtles that the Manus supplied for them and in exchange the Usiai bartered or traded sago, taro, fibrous bark for thread and rope making, betel nuts, pepper leaves, bags, leaves for mats, gourd lime containers, gum for caulking their canoes, dishes, oil containers, and most important, the wood that made it possible for the Manus to build their big vaulted houses and construct the fine and often large sail-topped canoes by which they were known everywhere in the archipelago. It was also known that most of the young men of Manus went away to work for two or three years on the plantations of the white man; and in Lorengau, the government station, before leaving for the south coast, Margaret had her first encounter with the Manus houseboys, and the curious "pidgin" that they spoke.

Pidgin, the language the Manus natives spoke, "a flexible flowing language with a cadence of its own," she found wonderful. "The words," she wrote, "come from everywhere, perhaps sixty percent are English. Five percent mission introduced, a few German, the rest picked up at random from various native tongues. . . . They use *me* for I, *fella* in front of every word as a sign that it's a noun—insert, *em* after every verb. —you look 'em, what name? (Means. What do you see?) You like make 'em line, you like make 'em paper?" (Would you like to join a line of boys and make a contract?)"

It was soon time to leave Lorengau and set off for the village of Peri, a large village that seemed suitable for the study to be made. For many reasons this stay would be different from Margaret's first experience in Samoa. The people of Manus were not nearly so amiable or so easy to get to know as the dignified, gracious Samoans had been. The physical way of life was much more difficult, living as they did on, and practically *in*, the sea. Their babies had to learn practically from birth how *not* to fall through the wide slats of the floors they played on into the waters below. (Though if they did fall their mothers seemed able to rescue them with a quick-as-a-flash technique.) In general the Manus' attitudes were not the relaxed and generally friendly ones of Samoa but were often hostile, fearful, suspicious, angry, due in part to their form of ancestor worship in which these dead spirits wielded great and magical powers over the living. All of this meant that a sojourn with the Manus could be a trying experience for an anthropologist who was not specially prudent or sensitive to their feelings and ways.

But Margaret Mead and her husband felt ready for the challenge and prepared themselves for the long trip by sea to the appointed village. And Margaret ended her first letter this way:

. . . On Monday, Gizikuk, the chief of the soda-water (sea) boys, the Manus true" [as these people called themselves] "is coming to get us and our gear in a fleet of canoes. We'll have an all day trip along the coast. By next letter we'll be in the thick of it. I've already got a fair start on the language. Boat every three weeks.

Kwe bo kua. You may go.

Margaret

The "gear" that they had assembled to go with them was not nearly so elaborate as one might imagine for such a project. They had two stretchers, two tables, two chairs, a typewriter, a camera, developing apparatus, a shotgun, rice and tobacco in bulk (for gifts), and, most important for Margaret Mead's plans—baubles by the gross: beads, toys, balloons, paper flowers, and a thousand sheets of paper for the children to draw on, which proved to be quite insufficient, for it was used up in a month. No more than these things, for the good ethnologist knows how important it is to slip as quietly as possible into the routine of native life and in that way to make the presence and arrival of an inquiring white person as inconspicuous as possible.

Gizikuk, the so-called headman of the South Coast Manus and the one man who was able to make the ten independent little democracies that existed supply needed canoes for the government, arrived and was presented with "grease"—in this case 20 sticks of tobacco. But he said that the expedition would require at least nine canoes. By Dr. Mead's estimate four and a half would have been plenty. But at this delicate point of encountering a new people, it was wisest not to make issues; and on the long trip to the village of Peri, while the crew cooked and ate messes of sago and coconut oil, the anthropologists sat famished. It was best to rely on the eventual hospitality of their native hosts than to risk insulting them and perhaps delaying for weeks or months the work they had come to do. An ethnologist must always act with the greatest care in such situations.

It was not till midnight, as Margaret later recalled, that they arrived at Peri. ". . . the fleet of canoes under full sail swept into the moonlit lagoon village, between the rows of pile-built houses and up to the doors of the 'House Kiap,' the government barracks where we took up our temporary abode." A few weeks later she wrote exultantly to "Papa Franz" (Professor Boas):

It's hard to imagine more favorable working conditions; a possible climate with few mosquitoes, decent food, complete isolation from white people and mission influences, an open-hearted people. The children are independent little water rats. Children of four swim an eighth of a mile with big knives in their teeth. . . .

The tall arched houses of Peri set on their wooden stilts made Margaret Mead think of long-legged birds, particularly when the tide was low and the muddy bottom was visible. When the tide was high the children played on the slat verandas beneath the houses or sailed their small canoes between them. The only "land" about was the few tiny man-made islands and the mere dabs of green to be seen on them. Beyond in the open waters she watched the men and the older boys fish all the day long, using the split bamboo traps that allowed the fish to enter but not to leave, making them easy prey for the Manus fishermen to spear or shoot with bows and arrows.

Living in the small house that served as visitors' quarters while another larger habitation was being built for them at the other end of the village, Margaret Mead and her husband did the groundwork that had to be done if they were to know and understand the Manus people. They learned more of the language, became familiar with the intricacies of social organization, the economic customs, the religious beliefs and practices that made up the daily existence of the Manus and that were the framework within which their children grew up. The anthropologists became conscious too of who there was that might be trusted, and who perhaps it would be dangerous to displease.

Meanwhile their household staff grew. They added two more young boys to serve as cooks and general helpers in addition to the first two, a Manus school boy they'd found in Rabaul and another in the port of the Admiralties. Through their household staff the anthropologists let it be known throughout the village that they wanted to learn the language and to see all the important events in the lives of the villagers. "It was as if we had hung up a shingle saying, 'We want to be bothered. We aren't like other white people.' " And the Manus responded to the invitation with enthusiasm. The house was crowded with curious visitors from early morning till midnight.

Margaret Mead began to understand something of the many taboos of the Manus, all strongly observed, particularly those connected with marriage. The burdens of most of these taboos fell upon the women. Manus girls were usually engaged at five or six years of age even though the marriage ceremony did not take place for years after. But a woman must under no circumstance be seen by her husband's older male relatives nor by the husbands or fiancés of her younger female relatives. She must therefore spend most of her younger life hiding behind divider mats in the big houses, or muffling her face in her mat or cloth cloak. It took a while before Dr. Mead grew accustomed to seeing one of the women of the Manus sailing by the house of some taboo relative, her entire body and head lost in a great piece of cloth billowed out behind her by the wind.

There were, too, an endless number of taboos upon mentioning the name of any relative-in-law in a person's presence. This made it necessary, if one wanted to avoid breaking these taboos, to know the social organization of the village by heart, all the past marriages, the present marriages, and any marriages to come. And, it was necessary, to know the three or four names that belonged to each and every villager. And even so it was all too easy to make a mistake as Margaret Mead did once when she sneezed in the presence of a woman whose daughter was engaged to a young man named "Sneeze."

In mid-February Dr. Mead attended a Manus wedding and wrote home about it. ". . . The wedding was a gay affair badly mutilated by a rain storm. In the general scramble for positions I found myself assigned to the house of the bridegroom, which was the result of the taboos governing our various informants, but it turned out to be quite right for all the men fled the house of the groom after he had been ceremonially prepared for the great ordeal with elaborate anointing with red paint. The titular father of the groom simply remained to hand the bride hastily into his house; then he leapt into the bridal canoes which had brought her and was poled away. The little bride so laden with shell money, dog's teeth, bead-work, feather combs that her person was hardly visible sat at the top of the ladder with her back to the groom, who waited a moment and then made a rush for the back door. Whereupon all the groom's paternal aunts rushed at the bride, took the combs out of her hair, dug in her armlets for the several pipes which were concealed there. The girl was half-dead from embarrassment. Bethrothed years ago before, she had never been able to enter the village of her future husband. When she passed a village canoe she was forced to muffle her face in her cloak or pandanus rain shelter. Now at seventeen or so she was brought to the house of relatives at the far end of the village, decked out in all her finery, her ears heavy with bead earrings, her nose weighed down with a long dogs' teeth pendant. . . ."

The spirits of Manus, responsible for an atmosphere usually heavy with fear and terror, managed to make even the anthropologists' life difficult. In February Margaret Mead caught cold and had to stay in bed. Her little cook Kilipak came down with fever at the same time. A rash of illnesses and several deaths had raised the level of hysteria higher than usual. In Manus all sickness was attributed to the spirits. So it was no surprise to Margaret to receive a visit from a group of three of the village elders, headed by one who was very anxious to have the newcomers move at last into the still not finished new house he had built for them in his part of the village. They came to tell the anthropologists that they must move. Sori, the ghost of the old house site, they were told, was responsible for their illness. Margaret Mead tried to delay, but it was no use. In the next few days two more of the children in her house became ill, and so off they all went to the new house —still without steps, and the cookhouse still without walls or a floor, a veranda that was only a scaffolding.

But after a little while Margaret Mead found her new house charming. She described it in a letter: ". . . a bedroom filled with shelves . . . where the beds can remain all day instead of being folded up, a place to retire into to open treasure chests or take a sponge bath. Then there is a great big living room which I have decorated with native things. Round black water pots stand in pairs by two of the doors; two carved crocodiles sit upon the ridge pole and chat together, so the natives say, whenever we go out. On the green bamboo shelves are ranged carved wooden bowls. The shelves are curtained with pandanus mats, and the doors with mats also. The only foreign things are a few books, our tables and chairs which are natural wood and so blend well, a lamp and a tinkling glass Chinese gong which tinkles in the wind and delights the natives. . . . There are cedar wood chests on which the children draw. On my shelf is a basket, which belongs to the children; it contains pencils, crayons, erasers, scissors, coarse thread and needles for sewing up the sails of toy boats, a toy or two. . . ."

Dr. Mead's house was never empty of children. Since they were the principal subject of her investigations from a psychological as well as from an ethnological point of view, the arrangement of having children for servants worked out well. There was Banyalo, a schoolboy from Rabaul; the head cook named Manawei—which meant Bird—who had "dignity extraordinary"; there was Kilipak, the head cook, who was a son of the ruling family and a natural leader of men. These older boys, who were about 14, attracted all sorts of other children to the premises, many of them to serve as helpers, or "monkeys"—Manus pidgin for a small boy. The older ones in turn often delegated the disagreeable aspects of his task to a six-year-old. "Dinner was often prepared by some dozen small hands, one small boy tending each pot, faithfully blowing up the twig fire underneath. The little girls were enlisted to pluck the wild pigeons and to fetch the fire wood," reported Margaret Mead in a long diary-letter.

She asked all the children, whether they worked in the house or came to visit, to make drawings. These were an important way of learning about the children's feelings about their lives, themselves, the people around them, the environment in which they lived. And the children were so enthusiastic about this occupation that "every available square inch of table, box, or trunk surface was pre-empted by children engaged in drawing. They would have drawn all night happily had I permitted them, and they came to wake me before dawn with requests for 'paypa.' "

It was also possible for Margaret Mead to watch the children at play from behind the shelter of the thatched walls of her house. From there she could see them on the wide verandas, on the little island adjoining her house, or canoeing in the wide lagoon or through the "streets," the waterways of the "primitive Venice" that the village of Peri was. "Children of three and four," she wrote in a December 16, 1928, letter to Ruth Benedict, "can pole canoes ten times their size, handling a pole ten feet high. The three and four year olds have tiny canoes of their own, in which they paddle about half under water, upsetting every other minute, perfectly at home. . . . It's a paradise for children. They have no work except to run errands, and that involves paddling about in the water. The women take care of the babies so that the children are free. At low tide in the early morning they course about shooting fish with tiny bows and arrows, dragging the water for minnows with a long piece of bark used in imitation of a net, or practicing just missing the other's feet with pieces of coral hurled through the water. . . ."

At other times Dr. Mead took part in the festivities and ceremonies of the whole village. She rode in the big canoes, went to the feasts, watched in the house of mourning, and sat severely still while the mediums spoke with the spirits of the dead. A few times, at the risk of angering the entire village, she and her husband served as doctors when the children fainted from malaria or some other cause—using no ministrations more complicated than a bottle of spirits of ammonia.

Slowly Margaret Mead became familiar with the Manus language, which was strange and hard to pronounce—"a mass of sounds which are intermediate between sounds familiar to us and a great deal of individual variation." She got so that she could joke in it and at times even pun a little. She learned to shudder when taboos were violated, or to meet the news of a misfortune with the question, "Which ghost is responsible?" In short, she had come to feel partly like one of the Manus people. And now it was becoming possible for her to recognize not only these characteristics of this people that made them different from the culture from which she came, but also those that, to her surprise, were amazingly similar.

The worship of ghosts, the physically demanding and primitive way of life, the strange costume of the people, their undisguised fears and reactions—all these things created the impression of a people far removed from those who lived in New York City or Chicago, or perhaps in the suburbs of any great American metropolis. But now Margaret Mead had begun to look beneath the surface, into the inner values that really dictated the pattern of Manus life. There she saw some striking parallels. Where Samoa, she thought, had been able to shed light on American culture by its different approach to life, Manus it seemed would be able to teach us through the ways in which it was like our own society.

What was most important to a Manus man? The amassing of dogs' teeth—the Manus form of money—not as in America to put in the bank or to buy stocks with, but to hang round his neck or the necks of his children, to buy a bride for his sons, to trade for food, to buy precious articles from other peoples of the peninsula. What did he consider the most important lessons to impart to his children? Aside from the essential physical training of the young child in swimming and canoeing which made even a Manus baby quickly able to survive the dangers of living over the lagoon, Manus adults taught their children the value of private property so well that even the tiniest children would not touch any object left within their reach unless they were certain that they might have it for themselves.

Marriage among the Manus had many of the same problems that American marriages, still feeling the effect of the Victorian era, had. Men and women did not love each other freely. There was an atmosphere of shame between them, instilled partly by taboos, and a rigid almost puritanical approach among them that made any sort of dishonesty—especially in business—a sin sure to be punished by death or illness through the intervention of the Manus spirits. This had an aura not far removed from the one that existed in old New England at the time of the Salem witch trials.

It was from watching the Manus children, however, that she learned most. As she reported a year later in her book, *Growing Up in New Guinea*, ". . . Those who believe that all children are naturally creative, inherently imaginative, that they need only to be given freedom to evolve rich and charming ways of life for themselves, will find in the behaviour of Manus children no confirmation of their faith. . . ." For from the drawings she had gathered together from the Manus children she came to the conclusion that "If the chil-

dren's imaginations are to flourish they must be given food."
By this she meant a strong cultural heritage of the kind seen
in Europe and in the United States. "The great majority of
children will not even imagine bears under the bed unless the
adult provides the bear." Dr. Mead also saw how the Manus
children, though given no training or education for the sort of
adult life they would have to lead someday, nevertheless did
manage to adopt the adult culture when the time came; and so
it seemed to her that people in the United States tended to
overvalue the educational process, believing that a child can
be changed and taught anything in school, and undervalued
"the iron strength of the cultural walls within which any individual can operate."

But the parallel that emerged most strongly for Dr. Mead
between the children of Manus and those of upper-class and
middle-class America was the amazing lack of responsibility
fostered in the children of both groups. Manus children were
dreadfully pampered. They were allowed to play all day long
with nothing in the way of tasks required of them. They soon
became so spoiled that she observed on occasion a child who
would hit or punch its mother if she refused him anything,
and she saw even quite tiny children, who when they were tired
would insist that their more tired mothers carry them on their
backs. To their fathers, the leaders of Manus society by virtue
of their wealth, the children did not show any real respect.

She believed this glaring lack of respect for elders that
she felt also existed in the American home came from the same
cause. For in the United States, as in Manus, a man was valued not for what he was or for what he could do but mainly
for what he owned and could buy—in short for how much
money or how many dogs' teeth he possessed. She laid down

the principle in her book that "we can expect to have no real discipline and hence no real dignity until we shift our valuations from having to being. When the emphasis of a society is upon what people are as individuals then dignity is in that people." As she had seen in Samoa, it seemed to her that Americans might learn a very important lesson from Manus: in order for the culture to be rich and a true gift to pass on to the children, it is the adults who must create a worthy tradition. Otherwise, Margaret Mead implied, American adults were, like the adults of Manus, certainly failing their most precious responsibility—to their children. For "To treat our children as the Manus do, permit them to grow up as the lords of an empty creation, despising the adults who slave for them so devotedly, and then apply the whip of shame to make them fall in line with a course of life which they have never been taught to see as noble or dignified—this is giving a stone to those who have a right to good bread."

When Margaret Mead left Manus at last, she had grown fond of the people of the island after their many months together. And the Manus had grown fond of her. They beat the ceremonial drums sounded for the dead and for those who depart from Manus forever. It seemed certain to them that this woman, who had come to them from so very far away, would never return. It seemed equally unlikely to Margaret. For no prophecy occurred to her, not even in her most aware and scientific self, to suggest what the future would bring. A terrible war would change the face of the world, speed up the inevitable process of culture-contact between her own complex civilization and far less complex ones like that of the Manus—and in her role as anthropologist she would find herself again, many, many years later, once more among the Manus.

Chapter *8*

The Many Ways of Men and Women

Margaret Mead returned from Manus in September 1929 eager to write up her findings as quickly as possible and get back to the field. Her father had predicted there would be another world war in ten years. "Sister," he had once said to her, "you have just 20 years before another war." Right after her return, there had been the big crash in Wall Street. The bank failures and the stock market crash affected many of Margaret's friends; but she was no gambler and had refused to invest the money she had made from *Coming of Age in Samoa* in the stock market, preferring to save it as a nest egg towards her next field trip. She was much more concerned with the long term issues—the disappearing primitive cultures of the world—than she was with the immediate financial situation of the United States. Haunted by the thought of how much work there was still to do in order to record the ways of these few remaining untouched societies before another war would come to change and in many cases obliterate their highly individual patterns, she set to work furiously organizing her notes and writing them up into articles, books, scientific reports.

In the American Museum of Natural History she had much to do cataloguing the collection of specimens she had brought back with her from Manus, and supervising the preparation of an exhibition of them to be put in the great South Sea Hall. She had to select photographs, have labels printed, supervise the construction of a miniature Manus village. This diorama—as such miniatures are called—was a perfect replica of the tall thatched houses, the elegant big-sailed canoes, the fishing and cooking equipment used in the village of Peri. During the first winter after her return, she wrote most of her book *Growing Up in New Guinea*.

Sometime in the middle of the winter, Dr. Clark Wissler, Curator of Anthropology of the American Museum of Natural History, asked Margaret Mead if she would do a study of women on a reservation of American Indians in the United States. This idea did not appeal to her at all, for she was eager to hurry back to her still pure cultures in the Pacific area. But it was the first—and only—time the Museum ever gave her a direct field assignment. A grant had been obtained by the Museum from Mrs. Leonard Elmhirst for this particular purpose. And since Margaret Mead was one of the few women anthropologists in the United States and on the staff of the Museum, she felt that in all fairness she had to do it.

She spent the following summer living with an American Indian tribe whose culture was so broken and whose lives were so deteriorated that she not only disguised the names of individuals in the tribe—as she had done in her book on Samoa—but she changed the name of the tribe itself. In the book she wrote about her research among them, *The Changing Culture of an Indian Tribe,* she called them the Antlers, which was not their real name at all. And she described in this book what happened to members of a society when it was in the last stage of upheaval and change because it had come into such close and continuous contact with white civilization and all its "progress." In a letter to Ruth Benedict, written July 21, 1930, Margaret mentioned some of the problems she was up against that were making her work difficult.

"This is a very discouraging job, ethnologically speaking. You find a man whose father or uncle had a vision. You go to see him four times, driving eight or ten miles with an interpreter. The first time he isn't home, the second time he's drunk, the next time his wife's sick, and the fourth time, on the advice of the interpreter, you start the interview with a $5 bill for which he offers thanks to Wakanda, prays Wakanda to give *him* a long life, and proceeds to lie steadily for four hours. This is the more usual procedure . . . before anyone will open their mouths, and one or two cases where people will talk through corruptibility. But they know so little. Practically everything stopped in the days of the old men's fathers."

At last, by the following summer, Margaret felt she was really ready to set off again to do her own work in the Pacific. She had worked hard since her return from the Admiralty Islands, as she recalls, "writing in the daytime, going over notes in the evening, a few lecture trips, a little teaching, hurry, hurry, hurry to get back." In less than two years she had produced two books, a variety of scientific papers, she had installed the Manus collection in the Museum, and she had done the American Indian field work. She had done a lot of thinking, too, about the subject of her next project, and had come to the conclusion that this time she would have to start her observations of the education of children still further back than she had before now—with infants rather than adolescents (as she had in Samoa) and than young children (as she had in Manus). She would also have to choose a problem to focus her field-work, for she believed this was the way to make ethnological research count.

The question of sex as a factor in the shaping of character was in the minds of many people. And to Margaret Mead it seemed logical and important to try to find out how various societies interpreted the basic temperament of their peoples in terms of sex: what is meant, in other words, in different societies, to be a man, or to be a woman. She hoped, that by carefully watching the way in which the babies were born and handled and nursed and weaned in different simple groups, she would be able to get some fairly clear idea of how those babies were being molded, though of course they were too young to know it, to fit the image of what their own society believed it meant to be a boy or to be a girl. In her own society almost everyone had very definite ideas of what was "boyish" or girlish"; but in her past investigations Margaret had found "human nature" to be far more varied than Western society assumed it to be. Once again she suspected that reality might upset the popular applecart of accepted ideas.

Again, Margaret Mead was all ready to leave. Then a review written by a leading senior anthropologist accused her of having a superficial knowledge of Manus culture and particularly of the ways in which the kinship system—the system of relationships based on marriage and birth—was organized in Manus. This review so infuriated Margaret that she postponed her trip for three more months to stay in New York and write a more complete description of a kinship system than anyone had ever written. It was called *Kinship in the Admiralties*. Later on Margaret commented: "Fury at being misunderstood is a very useful emotion if it can be kept impersonal, and channelled into writing monographs rather than into bitter scientific fights."

At the end of August 1931, she sailed with her husband by way of the Panama Canal for their next destination—the Sepik Aitape District of northeastern New Guinea, an area with a great variety in the local landscape: mountains, plains, lakes, big and little rivers. Here many highly individualized tribes lived, still holding to the core of their customs, a condition that made them ideal small laboratories for the work Margaret Mead planned to do among them.

This region, however, was in many ways a more dangerous one than any Dr. Mead had spent time in before. Many of the peoples had until very recently been cannibals and headhunters. Though they were now supposed to be under control of the Australian authorities, they were only lightly watched over, and if angered or upset their actions could hardly be guaranteed. As an anthropologist, Margaret Mead's principal fears had never been for herself; but like most enthologists, who accept the hazards that often accompany fieldwork, her greatest worry was that the notes and materials she collected might be destroyed. To protect not only these materials, but her own role in the work, and to make sure that the project would be completed, Dr. Mead always tried to avoid anything that might cause disaster, and to be as careful as possible within whatever risky situations she encountered.

In Samoa, the hurricane, the ocean, the great reef were unavoidable perils that she learned, more or less, to accept. And this knowledge helped her later on when she lived among the Manus in the tall houses built over the water, although she had never learned to swim. Now on this field trip she had to develop special techniques to deal with the undisciplined emotions of the New Guinea people. For she came to understand that had she ever relaxed a rule she made, or broken a tribal taboo, or permitted infringements of her property or authority, she would "have been dead within a few weeks." Still her overall philosophy towards possible mishaps during her work in the field was and is that "expeditions and adventures are mutually incompatible," and that "disasters are the results of haphazard planning and inept procedures."

With her anthropologist husband without whom she would not have dared go to so difficult an area, she set off for the quite unknown regions of northern New Guinea. They made as much careful preparation beforehand as they could manage without really knowing what conditions and peoples they would actually meet there. Dr. Mead could hardly have known, for instance, that the schooner she was on would get stuck on a sandbank up the Sepik River with no small boat available to take them off, and that it would take a slight earthquake to shake the ship loose. Nor could she have guessed that her hair, which she had finally grown long, would keep coming down in the middle of another near shipwreck (with a crew that didn't know the coastline), and that she would cut her hair short, deciding long hair to be "incompatible with this kind of life." Unforeseen, too, was the fact that all but one white man encountered in the period during which Dr. Mead and her husband lived among the first tribe they studied, the Arapesh, would die a violent death.

They went first to an Arapesh village called Alitoa and stayed there because the villagers who carried the anthropologists' gear refused to go any farther than that mountain village. Because Alitoa had 24 houses in which 87 people could and did sometimes live, it was considered the largest village. In actuality only three families inhabited Alitoa reguarly. The village stood on a hill so steep that many of the houses jutted out over a sharp drop; and whenever there was a feast, men, women, dogs, and children could be found spilling over the edges of town and sleeping under the dripping eaves of the poorly thatched houses. Margaret soon understood why when an Arapesh mountain man referred to a feast he had been to, he said, "We were burned by the sun and washed by the rain. We were cold, we were hungry, but we came to see you."

She found the Arapesh a mild, though poor, group who had developed a society in which, while there was never enough to eat, each man spent most of his time helping his neighbor. And, though the mountain people were said to be sorcerers by the coastal people, the atmosphere in the hills was so peaceful that, as Margaret reported in her book *Sex and Temperament,* published several years later, the "women go about un-attended; pairs of tiny children stray along the paths, hunting lizards with their miniature bows and arrows; young girls sleep alone in deserted villages."

The Arapesh men were every bit as much as committed to the cherishing adventure of growing and nourishing everything —the land, the yams, the pigs, the coconut trees, their children—as were the Arapesh women. This community spirit was of great interest to Margaret Mead. Here *was* a difference in the interpretation of what it meant to be a man. And she learned that in the Arapesh language the verb meaning "to bear a child" was applied to men as well as women, for the Arapesh men shared full concern over the birth and bringing up of their children. After the baby was born, an Arapesh man man might lie down by his wife's side; and it would be said that he too was "in bed having a baby." Later he shared his wife's task of caring for the newborn child, and the baby's "life-soul" was believed to have come from either father or mother.

How did the Arapesh man, and woman for that matter, develop such a loving and pacific character? This, of course, was a natural question for an anthropologist making a study of how sex differences were expressed or not expressed in different societies. To try to answer it, Margaret Mead carefully watched the way the Arapesh reared their children. She saw that their babies were given a constant continuous warm sense of physical security. They were always held by their mothers against their bodies, or in little soft net bags that permitted the children to still feel the living bodies against which they rested. Later, when the children were able to walk and to run and therefore able to stumble and fall, she saw that Arapesh adults were careful to be there to prevent disaster; and in this way the little Arapesh learned to trust and to feel that "though this is a cold, wet world, full of pitfalls, hidden roots in the path, stones over which small feet stumble . . . there is always a kind hand, a gentle voice to rescue one."

Marriage among the Arapesh meant a strong, warm domestic attachment that was built gradually. Arapesh girls were betrothed when they were seven or eight years old to boys about six years older than they were, and went to live in these future husbands' homes. The youths were said to "grow their own wives," for the men assumed full responsibility for such little wives-to-be, who were given to them when small—as a "special small girl, whose hand must be taken in rough places on the paths." An Arapesh girl went to her marriage without fear or strangeness, accepting her husband's family as her own, and feeling that she could trust and depend on her young husband. Obviously the Arapesh preferred the safety of domestic love, sacrificing, by American standards, the thrills of romance and the excitement of the stranger with whom one falls in love on first sight.

"This is the texture, the pattern, of Arapesh life," Margaret Mead wrote in *Sex and Temperament*, "quiet, uneventful co-operation, singing in the cold dawn, and singing and laughter in the evening, men who sit happily playing to themselves on hand-drums, women holding suckling children to their breasts, young girls walking easily down the centre of the village, with the walk of those who are cherished by all about them."

But after seven months among the Arapesh, it was time to move on. The new people were quite a change from that first contented group to whom, as she wrote, "the world is a garden that must be tilled, not for one's self, not in pride and boasting, not for hoarding and usury, but that the yams and the dogs and the pigs and most of all the children may grow." Margaret Mead was off to the headhunting Mundugumors, who lived about 40 miles away.

"You are going up the Sepik River," she was warned by Arapesh elders just before she left, "where the people are fierce, where they eat men. You are taking some of our boys with you. Go carefully. Do not be misled by your experience among us. We are another kind. They are another kind. So you will find it."

And so indeed she found it. For the Mundugumor, a tribe of some 1,500 or so people who lived on the Yuat, a wild river with a "current so swift that a motorboat makes very little progress against it," were every bit as fierce as promised and offered an almost unbelievable contrast to the quiet Arapesh she had just left.

The Mundugumor tribe lived on both sides of the Yuat River, and both groups still spoke the same language. Once, however, they had lived on one side of the river; then the river had changed its course, separating the two groups for so long that they no longer felt themselves to be the same people, and periodically they ate each other. Quarrels, violence, fear dominated the Mundugumor scene. Dr. Mead knew that she had to be continually alert. "I moved about among the people easily," she recalled later on, "but I had to be careful not to get into a situation where I might seem too tempting—or let too many people up into the house at one time. . . . There was temporary peace in Mundugumor. The people were afraid that the government would punish headhunting by putting them in prison. But there was continual verbal strife. 'Just you wait until there are no white people about, and I'll finish you off,' the fiery younger brother of one of the two 'big men' would scream at him, brandishing a spear."

It was not difficult for Margaret Mead to see, before long, in the manner in which the Mundugumor treated their children, even in their attitude towards having children, where much of the difficult Mundugumor character came from. Most Mundugumor women did not want children and seemed to dislike them from birth. Babies were nursed, handled, and weaned in a harsh and abrupt way. They were rarely held in their mothers' arms, they were carried in stiff, hard baskets, they were nursed in uncomfortable positions and weaned by blows and cross words. Everything that happened to the Mundugumor baby, Margaret Mead saw, created the feeling of a hostile and dangerous world in which he must be equally tough if he wanted to survive. As might be expected, only the very strongest children did survive, and these were quickly taught a long string of elaborate prohibitions and rules—mostly having to do with a complicated kinship system that separated fathers from sons, made them rivals for the attentions and favors of the Mundugumor women. The Mundugumor women were as aggressive in their own way as the Mundugumor men were, and they fought and chose their own mates as often as they were chosen. An atmosphere of violence and anger prevailed between men and women, not ending even after marriage and the birth of children.

In this small world where fierceness reigned, what happened, Margaret Mead wondered, to the "deviant," the misfit —the man or woman who does not conform to the accepted personality of his society? In the case of the Mundugumor, how does the man or woman who would like to cuddle a baby, or help his neighbor, or cultivate a garden, fare?

Better than might be expected, Margaret Mead discovered; for beneath the violent level of Mundugumor society, a number of these nonconformists not only helped maintain some sort of stability, law and order; but they also, by cherishing a nonviolent ideal, kept the society from changing.

The Tchambuli, the third tribe in New Guinea that the anthropologists chose to study, were a small group of only 600, and they lived on a lake. The water of this lake, wrote Margaret, keenly sensitive to all she saw, "is so coloured with dark peat-brown vegetable matter that it looks black on the surface, and when no wind stirs it, resembles black enamel. On this polished surface, in still times the leaves of thousands of pink and white lotuses and a smaller deep-blue water-lily are spread, and among the flowers, in the early morning, the white osprey and the blue heron stand in great numbers. . . . When the wind blows and ruffles the black surface to a cold blue, the lotus-leaves that lay so inert and thick upon the enamel surface are ruffled, and lifting lightly along their stems, show themselves to be not a green monotone, but a variable rose and silver-green, and of a delicate and pliant thinness. The small sharp hills that edge the lake gather clouds upon their summits which resemble snow and accentuate their steep rise from the fen-land level."

It was no wonder, with writing as vivid as this, that the reading public bought Margaret's next book, *Sex and Temperament*, as delightedly they did their favorite novels, or that Ruth Benedict described it, "As fresh and unhackneyed as an exploration in Mars. . . . " For Dr. Mead was able to bring it glowingly to life on paper in all its reality for her less traveled public.

In many ways the Tchambuli culture was the most interesting of the three. Along the edge of the lake stood the ceremonial houses of the tribe; for as Margaret Mead soon learned, ceremony and theatricals lay at the heart of the Tchambuli culture. The Tchambuli men were, for the most part, artists and actors, skilled in dancing, carving, plaiting, painting, and were chiefly concerned with their role upon the stage of their society. On the other hand, the Tchambuli women spent most of their time inside the big houses they lived in—houses that held from two to four families—cooking, plaiting, mending their fishing gear, making the big mosquito baskets that other people in the area came to buy.

Before long Margaret realized that it was the women who actually dominated among the Tchambuli, and who had the economic power in their society. The women did the fishing, made the mosquito baskets, and managed the valuables. The Tchambuli men were dependent upon their women and lived in a "highly charged atmosphere of courtship," as Margaret described it, "in which no one knows upon whom a woman's choice will fall. . . . What the women will say, what the women will do, lies at the back of each man's mind as he weaves his tenous and uncertain web of insubstantial relations with other men." And how did the Tchambuli women rear their children? Tchambuli babies were "generously but nonchalantly" nursed "while [their mothers' fingers] were busy plaiting reeds into sleeping baskets or rain-capes." The women were warm but casual, and "as a group the Tchambuli women were jovial, solid . . . the most reliable aspect in the life of their artistic and uncertain men."

Now Margaret Mead had studied three groups within 100 miles of each other, each one incredibly different from the others. She had obtained material richer for her particular problem that she could ever have hoped for, and clearly she had proved that as far as masculinity and femininity were concerned, there was no such thing as a set "inborn human nature" that made all men everywhere in the world act one way, and women act another. For certainly the three primitive societies she had studied in New Guinea were a part of the same human race.

And there she had found a tribe where fathers were more tender than mothers, a group where the women were more dominant and executive-minded than the men—and all of these people were human beings. And theirs too was "human nature" —even where the qualities of men and women were the reverse of what our own culture considered masculine or feminine qualities—testifying, as far as Margaret Mead was concerned, to the fact that whatever "human nature" might be, it was beyond a doubt "almost unbelievably malleable."

To the bulk of people in the United States and Europe who firmly believed that the female sex was innately gentle, passive, motherly, loving, and so on, and that men were unchangeably aggressive, warlike, dominant, business-minded, and so forth, the publication of Margaret Mead's book, *Sex and Temperament,* in 1935 came as a shock. It neatly destroyed many cherished ideas of what it meant to be a woman and what it meant to be a man. In the light of her findings, Margaret Mead suggested that Americans might well take a deeper look at their own interpretation of masculinity and feminity—their traditional approach to courtship, the idea that all women are more generously endowed with maternal feeling than men, that men are naturally braver than women, that women tend to care more about peace than men do, and so forth. For one thing, she felt that these socially established ideas forced many people who could not conform to the so-called ideal traits for men and women to suffer, just as the "misfits" suffered in the New Guinea tribes. The boy who perhaps liked to cook or play with dolls, the girl who was interested in mechanics and technical matters was quickly made to feel that he or she was not acting "like a boy" or "like a girl."

Besides, it seemed to Margaret Mead that any society which insisted that any trait—love for children, interest in art, bravery in the face of danger—had to belong to one sex or another would not only upset the man or woman who did not fit the "ideal" picture, but would "penalize in greater or less degree every individual born within it," for "in practically every mind a seed of doubt, of anxiety is planted" and "almost every type of individual is left room to doubt" whether he or she possesses a really masculine or feminine nature.

Whenever a standard of behavior was imposed upon a group that ignored the different shadings and qualities of human personality, Margaret Mead believed the individual *and* the society suffered. At the end of *Sex and Temperament* she was to write: "If we are to achieve a richer culture, rich in contrasting values, we must recognize the whole gamut of human potentialities, and so weave a less arbitrary social fabric, one in which each diverse human gift will find a fitting place."

The waste of individuality always seemed tragic to her, who deeply believed in the supreme importance of the individual and in the sacred necessity for every individual to grow and reach, if possible, his or her optimum development. It seemed to her that only in this way, when each individual was permitted and encouraged to achieve his or her full growth, would any society be able to equal its own full potential and become as wonderful as she envisioned human society might someday be. And this version of a very bright future for the human race, one in which freedom, justice, and creativity would dominate the human scene in place of war, poverty, and fear, was a shining image Margaret Mead was never to give up.

Chapter 9

In Haste to Understand

Franklin Delano Roosevelt had been President for one year when, after two years in New Guinea, Margaret Mead returned to the United States in the fall of 1933. She came home alone. Five field trips and unremitting work had exhausted the resources of her marriage. Her husband returned to England and went on to work in China and a new marriage. The New Deal had just been started in an attempt to cope with the Depression and large-scale unemployment. The whole feeling in the country was one of change and experiment. Many of the people Dr. Mead knew were part of it. One of her younger sisters had a WPA (Works Progress Administration) job in Chicago, where her youngest sister was an administrative assistant in the Division of the Social Sciences. There was great concern about happenings abroad. The Nazis had taken power in Germany, Spain was in a political turmoil, the British were on the dole. And in response to the situation in Europe and the economic crisis at home, the political atmosphere in the United States was very open and liberal.

Margaret Mead, though conscious of the intellectual and political upheaval, was still intent on getting down the recent materials she had just gathered, writing them up as quickly as she could, and getting back to the field. For she still believed that "one of our best hopes of understanding ourselves and the other people in the world" depended on the gathering of information from groups like those she had just been with in New Guinea.

Again she lived in a brownstone house on 102nd Street, the same one she had lived in on her return from Manus. Again she spent her days at the American Museum of Natural History, organizing her field materials, cataloguing another big collection of artifacts, preparing them for exhibition. Again she was writing a book. This one would be called *Sex and Temperament*. And in addition, she was teaching one course, Culture and Personality, at Columbia University.

It was hardly possible for Dr. Mead to avoid contact with the various currents of left-wing thinking that were so prevalent in the academic and literary circles of New York City at the time. To many intelligent people, ideas of the far left, Socialism and Communism, seemed to be the only antidote for the growing strength of Nazism, Fascism, and other extreme right movements, and an economic cure-all for the appalling poverty rampant in the world. In retrospect, it seems to Margaret Mead that what saved her from joining the political radicalism of the day was her long association with her father's keen understanding of economic change, and a glimpse of the automation to come that would change Karl Marx's nineteenth century ideas so much that the main problem would be not how to produce enough goods but how to distribute them so that still more goods could be produced.

The same cold and snowy winter, Dr. Mead met Lawrence K. Frank, a man who had already done more to change the human sciences in the United States than any other. He invited her to share in a unique experiment he was planning—one that would bring the human and the social sciences together in a more complete and meaningful way than ever before. To do this Mr. Frank asked ten people who were experts in their own professions to come together at the Hanover Inn at Dartmouth College in New Hampshire to work together for one month and produce an outline of everything they knew about human development within society.

New Hampshire was warm that summer. As always, fine New England cooking was served at the Hanover Inn. The hills were very green, perfect for hiking, the nearby White River was cool and clear, wonderful for fishing and swimming. But members of the Hanover Seminar were far too busy to succumb to the abounding temptations.

Participants included Robert Lynd, author, with his wife Helen, of *Middletown*, a famous sociological study of an American city; Mark May and Hugh Hartshorne, whose studies of honesty in children had affected the public's thinking; Edna White, head of the Merrill Palmer School in Detroit; Mary Fisher, who ran the Vassar Institute of Euthenics, where Vassar girls a few years out of college brought their small children back to live in a children's dormitory while the mothers went back to school themselves to learn something about children. There was Lloyd Warner, just beginning to organize his famous series of books on Yankee City; Lura Beam, who, with Robert L. Dickinson, had made an intensive study of 1,-000 marriages; Edmund Day, later to become President of Cornell University; William Fisher, who taught literature at Sarah

Lawrence; John Dollard, just beginning to combine sociology, psychoanalysis, and learning theory at Yale University; James Plant, a psychiatrist who had started a school clinic to spot the children who were likely to go insane, and who found that with proper care such children turned out well instead. Then there was Lawrence K. Frank himself, "whose vision of unified knowledge and of a new form of education," it seemed to Margaret Mead, would embody "all that we were learning about culture, about child development, about human capacities and potentialities." And, of course, Dr. Margaret Mead.

Dr. Mead, having been reared by a sociologist (her mother), an economist (her father), and a grandmother deeply interested in methods of early childhood education, was fully aware of the other social sciences. The active, dynamic cooperation with a group of other scientists and scholars that began the summer of 1934 at the Hanover Inn marked a new phase in her professional life. Now there were new resources from the other disciplines to draw on in considering her own anthropological problems, any number of new ways her own findings could be used by the other sciences, infinite implications for the future of education, psychology, social planning, and so on. The whole venture was something like a symphony orchestra that succeeds in playing many exquisite and difficult pieces of music because of the joint efforts of many sensitive and highly trained musicians, each of whom knows and can play his own instrument with skill.

In the autumn of 1934, Dr. Mead finished *Sex and Temperament* and began a new project that grew out of the friendships of Hanover Seminar. This project involved one section of a big study on the nature of cooperation and competition. Students were very poor in those days, and Margaret Mead organized the project so that students were paid, instead of paying, to come to a seminar and help organize the materials for the study.

A book, *Cooperation and Competition Among Primitive Peoples*, in 1937, was the first attempt to relate the kind of character that children develop as they grow up in a particular society to the political and economic forms of that society. The plan for the book grew out of the people she worked with at Hanover and later friends made at this time: Geoffrey Gorer, who had just written *Africa Dances*, and had then decided to become a serious anthropologist rather than a writer who used materials about primitive peoples; Erik Erikson, who had recently come to the United States and was to become a leading child psychoanalyst; Kurt Lewin, a refugee from Hitler's Germany, who was to start what is called today group dynamics; Erich Fromm, psychoanalyst and sociologist, then working on family structure and human character; Karen Horney, a psychoanalyst who had not yet broken with the Freudians.

As coordinator of the study and editor of the book on cooperation and competition, Dr. Mead had many obstacles to surmount. There was no original material to answer the specific questions relating to cooperation and competition in the particular societies chosen for the study: the Arapesh, the Eskimo, the Manus, the Zuni Indians, the Dakota Indians, the Maori of New Zealand, and others. It was therefore necessary to embark on a sort of pioneer venture—a special kind of cooperation among graduate students, young field workers, and older field workers. They would try to put together existing material in such a way as to reveal individual and group attitudes in each society towards property, achievement, children and the aged, on how strong the development of the individual (the

[141]

ego) was in each culture, on the presence or absence of suicide.

And there was very little money to go round. "We had to create these materials," remembers Dr. Mead, "somehow, in the middle of a depression with a miniscule budget." Despite the difficulties, the book that resulted from the project was hailed as "a well-balanced summary of the nature and processes of group life . . ." in the *American Sociological Review;* and Dr. Mead herself felt the book paved the way for a future when perhaps "in the year 2010 we will still be asking new questions . . . questions grown urgent in the light of new forms of social organization on this earth and perhaps on other planets," and ". . . there will be no primitive peoples left to study."

At the end of the study of cooperation and competition, Margaret Mead's interest turned to another part of the Pacific, towards Bali, a small island off the mainland of Java in what is now Indonesia. She had become curious about the relationship between culture and the mental disease schizophrenia. The Committee for the Study of Dementia Praecox, as schizophrenia was called in those days, had been formed, and its director, Dr. Nolan Lewis, had asked various scientists including anthropologists how they would go about the study of schizophrenia. There were many reasons to believe that neuroses and psychoses were closely related to culture; and as the toll of schizophrenia continued to rise in the United States, it seemed more and more imperative to see what bases in childhood experience might contribute to this condition. Wasn't it possible that a culture might, in the way it formed the character of its people, cause, at least partially, schizophrenic behavior?

Dr. Mead had seen films of little Balinese girls in trance. Trance was a common occurrence in Bali. And she had been struck by what she had seen in a collection of drawings by the insane brought back from China. More and more she felt it would be important to go to Bali to look deeper into the problem of schizophrenia. Several other scholars were interested in research in Bali—Jane Belo, who had already lived in Bali and brought back films and photographs; Colin McPhee, who had been working on Balinese music; and Gregory Bateson, an English anthropologist who was interested in the relationship between culture and psychological types. And Dr. Mead hoped to explore, for the first time, the full value of photography as an aid in anthropological field work.

Margaret Mead left for Bali on a small freighter that carried only one other passenger beside herself. To avoid the Abyssinian War, still raging between Mussolini's Italy and Haile Selassie's small country, the little ship went round the Cape and took seven weeks before it reached Java. Dr. Mead, as always, made good use of her time working all day every day on a monograph on the Arapesh tribe. But she had one disaster. A page of her notes blew away while the freighter was anchored in a Sumatran harbor.

In March of 1936 Margaret Mead and Gregory Bateson were married, continuing in the tradition of their family backgrounds; for Mr. Bateson had been raised in an English home where he had been used to seeing his mother assist his father, a geneticist, in his work, not unlike the atmosphere Dr. Mead had known in her childhood home. And their own work in anthropology was complementary as well.

In Bali, for the first time, Margaret Mead was able to conduct her fieldwork without the customary hazards and discomforts of her past experiences. The Balinese were exotic, not primitive. The scenery was beautiful. There were plays and temple festivals and dances to attend—and to study. There were carvings and paintings to collect. The food was delicious. Wherever she'd worked before, she had always lost about 25 pounds. Not in Bali. Working conditions were ideal. It was a wonderful relief to be able to pay people to do things, rather than to have to persuade and cajole them. It was a joy for her to have a highly literate Balinese secretary named I Made Kaler (now head of a big school in Bali), and to be part of a highly trained and genuinely cooperative team. Dr. Mead took notes. I Made Kaler made a parallel text of the notes in Balinese. Gregory Bateson made photographic and film records. Later the texts had to be gone over, the thousands of photographs developed, the collections of carvings and paintings had to be catalogued.

A mountain village named Bajoeng Gede was chosen to be the base for most of the work done in Bali. The elements of early and pure Balinese culture were still to be found in Bajoeng Gede. The population was slow moving and accessible. Except for two later periods when Margaret and her husband lived first in a palace in Bangli, and later built a pavilion in the courtyard of a Buddhistic Brahman family in the village of Batoen, they stayed in Bajoeng Gede trying to see all the ways in which the Balinese people "as living persons, moving, standing, eating, sleeping, dancing and going into trance embody that abstraction technically called culture."

The color and charm of Balinese life moved Margaret Mead to write some of her most evocative descriptive passages. She began the text of the photographic study, *Balinese Character,* which she wrote with Gregory Bateson, thus: "Once every 400 days Bali is quiet and empty. The whole thickly populated section of the little island lies silent for the New Year, which is spoken of as the 'silence.' One can traverse the length of Bali, along the excellent roads which the Dutch have built, through village after village, between the long mud walls punctuated every few feet by the high narrow gates built in the distinctive style of that particular village, and see no women squatting before their own or someone else's doorway in front of an ankle high table covered with soft drinks and tidbits, no group of boys gambling for pennies, no cages of fighting cocks set out in the sun. The roads, at other times, are crowded with people coming and going from the markets, which are held every three days in the larger towns; crowded with people carrying rice, pulling carts loaded high with baskets or mats or pots being brought from a distance for sale; crowded with processions of people in silks and brocades, walking in easily broken lines behind their orchestras and their gods; gods represented by temporary minute images seated in small sedan chairs; gods represented by images made of leaves and flowers; gods which are masks or bits of old relics. With the processions mingle groups of people grimed from work, hurrying lightly beneath heavy loads; and theatrical troupes, their paint and fine costumes tucked away in little bundles, trudge wearily behind the two-man mask, the patron Dragon (Barong) who walks quietly with covered face.

But at the New Year these same roads are empty, stretching up and down the frequent hills. . . ."

But Dr. Mead's awareness of the beauty of Bali did not distract her from her purpose: to try to understand what it was that created the emotionally detached and formal character of the Balinese people. As always she looked for her answers to the children, and to their mothers. How were Balinese babies, considered at birth to be sacred and closest to heaven whence they had just come, treated? She and her husband's camera recorded the many ways in which a typical Balinese mother frustrated her child by teasing him, petting him, stimulating him to show love or desire or jealousy or anger, only to turn away as soon as the child began to respond to her. Balinese mothers were always fussing over someone else's baby in front of their own. They were continually threatening to leave their children or telling them that a stranger had come to carry them away. At a certain point, the Balinese child came to feel the only safety lay in impassivity, in never responding, in never rising to any lead. Fear, Dr. Mead identified as the emotion that principally shaped the character of the Balinese who, she later wrote "carries the memory of his mother's intense theatrical exclamation of fear, 'Aroh,' to deter him from ever venturing on an untrodden path."

The Tjalonarang, a traditional Balinese drama, was clearly an enactment of the parent-child relationship in Bali, usually played before an audience of solemn eyed children and impassive faced adults; children who watched the stage on which love and grief and aggression were played out though they themselves would probably never show those emotions again, for they had already withdrawn into themselves.

The central figure of the Tjalonarang is a witch. Dr. Mead felt she represented the Balinese mother and described her in *Balinese Character* as—"a masked supernatural being whose tongue is studded with flame, whose nails are many inches long, whose breasts are abhorrently hairy and pendulous and whose teeth are tusks," but, like the Balinese mother, she is not only a fear-inspiring character—as she is to her child— but she is herself afraid. As the drama goes on the witch is attacked by the emissary of the king and by the followers of the dragon. They all, however, fail to destroy her, and in their frustration they turn their daggers, powerless against the witch, against their own breasts. "Thus symbolically," wrote Margaret Mead, "they complete the cycle of the childhood trauma —the approach to the mother, the rejection, and the turn-in upon the self."

In the course of two years a complete record of interpersonal relations in Bali had been made. There were 28,000 photographs, and 22,000 feet of 16-millimeter film. Dr. Mead knew that they had succeeded in capturing a great deal of the nonverbal behavior of the Balinese people, and that when they returned to the United States it would not be necessary to rely only on memory for the image of the way a baby was held or bathed by its mother, or the expression on a child's face as it watched the witch in the Tjalonarang. Not only had they covered the ground they had planned to; they had such an excess of rich photographic material that another book, *Growth and Culture*, by M. Mead and Frances Cooke MacGregor with photos by Gregory Bateson, was written a few years later.

But the core of anthropological study is comparison, and Margaret Mead and Gregory Bateson suddenly realized they had no other culture to which to compare their work in Bali. Quickly they made the decision to go to the Iatmul tribe in New Guinea, about 600 miles to the East of Java. As he had done fieldwork among the Iatmul, and Dr. Mead was fluent in the *lingua franca*, the pidgin English that was spoken there, their work would be easier. They made preparations to leave and sailed from Surabaja to Port Moresby. On the trip from Bali to New Guinea they heard of Hitler's take-over of Austria.

Daily life among the Iatmul, a proud, tall group of headhunters who lived on the Sepik River and whose culture was not unlike that of the Tchambuli, was a good deal less comfortable than it had been in Bali. Crocodile hunting was a major occupation of the Iatmul that summer. Within the next eight months the anthropologists collected many notes, another 10,000 still photographs, and a lot more film. By using film in Iatmul as they had in Bali, they were able to set down in permanent form some powerful cultural contrasts. *Childhood Rivalry in Bali and New Guinea,* a film they made on their return proved to be unparalleled material for teaching purposes. And Dr. Mead felt more convinced than ever before of the value of such tools as movie cameras, and, later, tape recorders, instruments sensitive enough to supplement the "highly complex human instrument," the anthropologist, who in the beginning of anthropological research had been the only available instrument.

They were almost ready to return to the United States, when the difficult stint in Iatmul was over, but they returned to Bali to spend another six weeks rephotographing the babies who had been born while they were there, and who were almost a year older. It was March, 1939, before they were ready to sail. They had been away from home for over three years.

What had been learned in Bali and Iatmul? Had the study been worth all the work and struggle involved? Were there answers for the curious outsider who wanted to know why anthropologists bothered to go to all these out-of-the-way places, and to whom men and women like Margaret Mead and Gregory Bateson and their colleagues seemed strange and even absurd, choosing to live as they did for years in mosquito-infected huts, eating odd and often distasteful foods, risking violence and mishap, enduring dysentery and malaria?

On the ship taking Margaret Mead and Gregory Bateson back to the United States, they learned by ship's radio that Hitler had marched into Prague. The future was clear. War!

Two years were to go by before the United States would join her European allies in the battle against Nazism. Gregory Bateson's country England, would be at war within a few months. The world was about to change more drastically in a few years than it had in centuries. Boundaries would be wiped out. Little nations would disappear—absorbed by larger ones —their own identities obliterated. Great numbers of people would be annihilated. Above all, before peace was to return to the world again, a new weapon would be used that would present a problem of unparalleled solemnity to the people of the planet Earth.

It was becoming clear. Margaret Mead and other anthropologists began to see how unbelievably necessary and significant the work they had been doing all these years really was. Not for nothing had Dr. Mead gone into the jungles, sailed dangerous seas, sat cross-legged on the floor, learned seven native languages, developed her memory and endurance, sharpened her senses so that she could remember the way an Arapesh man held a digging stick, or a Samoan *taupo* danced. Not for nothing had she and her fellow anthropologists hurried, hurried, hurried to the last little corners of the globe now made inaccessible by war, to places where small groups of men and women had lived simpler existences. For not only progress but war was drawing the human race perilously close together. The world was truly one and the study of Balinese culture did have meaning for the mentally ill everywhere. It was no longer necessary for anthropologists to prove the need for modern man and primitive man to understand each other and to see the common human ground they all shared. The major task of anthropologists had been to try to acquire understandings of the complicated human creature known as man. Those understandings were about to be called upon.

Chapter 10

Anthropologists in World War II

When Dr. Mead returned to the United States, she was determined, since the conflict with Nazism was inevitable because Hitler believed it necessary to destroy half the world and conquer the rest, to contribute all the understandings and skills she had to the job of winning the war. To keep "even the most humble talent wrapped in a napkin" seemed to her particularly reprehensible in such a time of emergency. Gregory Bateson had already gone to England to work on problems of morale for his country, soon to suffer daily bombing by Nazi planes. Margaret Mead had planned to go with him, but a very important reason, once discovered, made them both decide it would be best for her to remain in the United States. For pregnant women can be a burden under difficult wartime conditions, and Dr. Mead learned that she was soon to have a baby.

This new event in Margaret Mead's already adventurous life was a very happy one. She had always wanted to have children—at one time she had hoped to have six—but several doctors had told her in 1926 that she would never to able to carry a baby through an entire pregnancy, that she would always miscarry. (On hearing such news she had informed Professor Boas that he was free to send her anywhere in the field that he would send a man, for she did not have to be considered a woman to be given any special protection.) But years later she came to believe that perhaps she could have a baby after all, even though under the strenuous conditions of fieldwork she had never been able to. New medical discoveries, however, such as the Ascheim-Zondek test, which reveals pregnancy in a very early stage, and the value of vitamin E for helping to avoid miscarriage made it possible for Dr. Mead to have her baby. A girl, Mary Catherine Bateson was born on December 8, 1939.

Now Dr. Mead who had held and played with and observed so many children of so many different human communities had one all her own. She recalls, "I enjoyed my baby enormously, and everybody else did too," for Cathy as she was called, was reared in a world full of people, Margaret Mead's friends and colleagues. Dr. Mead recalls learning "a lot about mothers by being one, but not a lot about children. Having one child meant that I wasn't as good an observer as I had been because now all children were older or younger, or quicker or slower, or something—than mine." Naturally she related many of the things she had seen and learned about rearing children in other cultures—in Samoa, Manus, New Guinea, Bali, and in the United States—to her own child. "Mary Catherine was a self-demand baby before the word was coined. I tried to see that she was never in a strange place with a strange person; that she had a chance to learn to know and to trust many people of different skin color and appearance.

When she was two we moved to share a house with a large family of children so that she had foster brothers and sisters. . . ."

But although Margaret Mead found her daughter "a continuous delight," the gravity of the war demanded that Dr. Mead fill many roles as well as that of mother. What could an anthropologist do to help win a war? In the middle of the twentieth century, warfare had become something quite different from what it had been in the past. Scientific thinking now played its part in many ways, and the government of the United States realized that the findings of anthropologists and an anthropological point of view could be of very real help to the war effort. Soon Dr. Mead was at work for various government agencies. She became Executive Secretary of the Committee on Food Habits of the National Research Council, working, among other things, on problems of applied social change, trying to find ways to get the American public—and later other populations—to accept and use new nutritional findings. She bent her efforts to preserving democracy and preparing for a postwar world. She and other anthropologists, not always in an official government capacity, spoke out in an effort to clarify one of the most crucial issues of the war, Hitler's deadly racist myth, in the name of which millions of innocent people were being put to death. As Dr. Mead later wrote in the introduction to a postwar book, anthropologists felt that it was absolutely imperative to explain the truth about "just how individuals, born into a particular society, became members of its culture regardless of their initial racial inheritance or the culture in which their ancestors had lived. Unless we could spell out step by step, how a human baby, capable of learning any culture, learned completely to be a member of one culture, the racist myth, with its dangerously appealing and glib generalizations, its easy reliance upon the comforts of physical similarity, its irresponsible disposal of three-quarters of the world, might prevail."

But it was in the study of national character that Dr. Mead and other ethnologists made probably their most important contribution. Many years of contact with primitive groups made it possible for them to apply what they knew of the relationship of character to culture, particularly to the task of understanding the character of the people of the enemy countries, Germany and Japan. These studies helped the United States government wage what was called psychological warfare. This involved the preparation of propaganda, trying to predict enemy reactions to news and to allied moves, and understanding the behavior of enemy prisoners. One very important result of anthropological research was the decision by United States leaders to accept the recommendations made by anthropologists not to demand the deposition of the Emperor of defeated Japan. Geoffrey Gorer led the way in studies of Japanese character that caused anthropologists to believe that the core of Japanese society would be destroyed were the Emperor to be deposed or killed, leaving no one to direct affairs or to surrender.

Better understanding of America's allies also proved helpful. When, for instance, American GI's were stationed in England for long periods of time, differences in behavior, in attitudes, in ways of saying things sometimes caused tensions between the two nationalities. Americans thought the British arrogant. The British thought the Americans boastful. The British expected young men to carry much of the burden of good behavior. The Americans expected the British girls to do so. The British believed in coping—meeting difficult conditions by a stiffening of moral purpose. The Americans believed in fixing the conditions. Dr. Mead and other anthropologists tried to explain the two groups to each other. She went to England to lecture under the auspices of the Office of War Information in 1943, and she wrote pamphlets and special brochures for the military forces. This sort of interpreting was often of very real service.

She played many other no less important roles during the war. She tried to see that various highly trained scientists whom she knew were placed in strategic positions, where their knowledge could be put to best use. Almost everyone that Dr. Mead knew was now taking part in the war effort. Gregory Bateson returned to work first on morale, then on an analysis of enemy propaganda films, then in the Office of Strategic Services. Geoffrey Gorer, who had worked in the Office of War Information in the spring of 1942, later shifted to British Political Warfare. Ruth Benedict replaced him in the Office of War Information. Professor Boas, who had almost retired in 1937 from all activities after a series of personal tragedies "flung himself back into the world," as Margaret Mead later wrote in *An Anthropologist at Work*. He was ". . . roused by tremendous anger at Hitler's successes standing for every evil against which he had fought all his life—the denial of freedom and of universal human values," Professor Boas had devoted himself to all kings of anti-Nazi activities; writing, organizing committees, finding positions for scholars exiled from Ger many, providing materials for the German underground. "Tirelessly," wrote Dr. Mead, "he devoted what had seemed to be waning strength to the battle." Then ". . . on December 29, 1942, Boas was giving a lunch [for an old friend of his] at the faculty club at Columbia University. A glass of wine in his hand, he said, 'I have a new theory about race . . .' and fell back dead."

Ruth Benedict took on new responsibilities with Professor Boas' death. Her thinking had been deeply influenced by his. For a time she had filled his place in the Columbia University Department of Anthropology in 1937. In an obituary published in *The Nation,* Dr. Benedict briefly traced his life with its constant emphasis on social responsibility. "At eighty-four," she wrote, "he had not sold out or stultified himself or locked himself in a dogmatic cage. . . . After his retirement as head of the Department of Anthropology at Columbia University in 1936, he only felt himself freer to work to preserve those ideals for which we are fighting today. He was a great man, and at this moment we have need of such as he."

Ruth Benedict too had been swept into the struggle and had committed herself to take part in the war as an anthropologist. She too lectured and wrote about race. The work she did directly for the government was only a small part of her efforts. Her study of Japanese character was to result in a beautiful and important book, published in 1946, *The Chrysanthemum and the Sword.* At the same time, however, she was engaged, as were many anthropologists including Margaret Mead, in searching for the causes of war. The studies of culture that Dr. Benedict had made mostly with American Indians of the Southwest enabled her to look deeply into the problem. In a manuscript written in 1939, but never published, called A Natural History of War, she called war "an old plant on this earth," which "under modern conditions is socially disastrous to conquered and conqueror alike. . . ." In some tribes, she observed, war was considered "murder" and was punishable as such; while in others, closer in attitude to our own, it was considered "homicide with glory." But she completely discarded the idea that war was an inevitable accompaniment of being human. "It is a complete misunderstanding to lay this havoc to any biological need of man to go to war. The havoc," she wrote, "is man-made."

As the war continued, Margaret Mead's voice grew more and more familiar to Americans. She spoke on many subjects to many groups in the United States and abroad. Her name appeared with regularity in magazines and newspapers. She had important things to say. As Executive Secretary of the Committee on Food Habits of the National Research Council, she had the job of spreading information about modern nutrition, and she wanted if possible to reach even "the last woman down the road" who might not read or listen to the radio. Margaret Mead's voice was a positive one in a time of tension. She was capable of telling Americans many things pertinent to their well-being and safety without being an alarmist, without spreading fear. When this country first entered the war, Britain was being bombed, and no one in the United States knew whether or not American cities might not also be raided. Many families were apprehensive. In an article, "Proof Against Any Bomb," in 1942, Dr. Mead wrote from her experiences with primitive tribes where children were not shielded from disaster or death that she believed American children too could survive "scenes of death and terror" were they to come, if their parents and teachers were to remain "courageous and serene," as British parents and teachers had been even among falling bombs. "If you are to keep the children safe from fear," counseled Margaret Mead in the same article, "you yourself must be unafraid."

Despite fighting a war and rearing an infant daughter, Margaret Mead found time during a brief vacation soon after Pearl Harbor to write another book, *And Keep Your Powder*

Dry, published in 1942. She felt that the people of this nation at war needed to be made aware of their own national character and of what their special strengths were as a democratic nation. "As Americans . . . interested in winning the war and creating a just and honorable peace, it is as urgent that we recognize what we are ourselves as it is for us to understand the values and structures of other cultures." Dr. Mead told Americans that, in her opinion, they were essentially a moral people believing in right and wrong; and she set down many other aspects of American character recognizable to her readers and stated that she considered it terribly important that Americans fight and win *as* Americans, for "freedom's battles," she said, "must be won by freedom's own children."

At the same time she spoke out in many places of her concern for the youth of America and her fear that the younger children of freedom, particularly those in their late teens, were not being made to feel that there was a role for the individual in the social process of American democracy. "It is not enough to tell them that democracy is something they should be willing to die for in battalions unless we are also able to tell them that living for it individually is worth while," said Dr. Mead in "Youth Can Be Valiant,," in the *National Parent Teacher* in October 1941." She worried lest the Fascist approach with its emphasis on individual power and its leader-cult might triumph over a democracy that stressed materialism, worldly success, and technological advance as its primary goals, and that seemed to say what individuals did really was not significant, that they were merely pawns in the historical process. She urged in the same article that young people be made newly aware of the real premises of democracy in which ". . . Man choosing, willing and acting can shape his fate," because "History is in the making. Nobody has written the script." She told educators it was not enough merely for them to believe in democracy, but that "they must believe in the separate and individual worth of the human being."

The years of war went on for Margaret Mead in dedication, hard work, and the joy of seeing her little girl grow up. Cathy Batson began nursery school at two years old. And later, when she was ready for school, Dr. Mead helped to found a school where she could experience some of the things her mother felt were particularly important: being with children of different races and religions and classes, learning to paint from an artist and not an art teacher, establishing contact with other languages, and recognizing that our alphabet wasn't the only alphabet.

Then, with the Allied invasion of Europe, the uncertain balance shifted. Nazi conquests were halted at last, and their forces began the slow inevitable retreat. Germany and the countries she had swallowed were shattered by Allied bombs. Hitler and the last of his military hierarchy hid in a cellar waiting for the Allied troops to march in. In the Pacific, battles continued to be fought painfully on scattered islands. The struggle with Japan was long. Then finally, shockingly, with the dropping of two atom bombs on two Japanese cities, that conflict too was ended—and the war was over.

Chapter 11

Postwar: Ultimatum and the Challenge to Change

T he war was over, but Margaret Mead continued her work on many fronts. Some of the projects she had undertaken during the emergency of wartime were now required to meet the needs of the postwar world. This was particularly true of the study of national character begun primarily as a study of enemy countries, but which seemed in the postwar world even more important to meet the new challenge. While the control of atomic energy could mean that the human race might free itself from poverty and unnecessary labor, it might also mean the end, or near-end of the human race itself. The bombs dropped on Hiroshima and Nagasaki offered the world an ultimatum. The different peoples and nations of the earth would now have to find some way to live on the same planet in harmony, or perish. So the task of understanding, for which anthropologists in particular were so well trained, was even more imperative than it had been ever before in man's history.

During World War II, Margaret Mead had persuaded Dr. Ruth Benedict, her friend, teacher, and colleague, to join her in the first efforts to apply anthropology to international understanding. In 1946, Ruth Benedict returned from her Washington, D.C., job to Columbia University in New York City to inaugurate a study of European cultures and to begin a battle to have the new methods necessary to "study culture at a distance" recognized. Many of these new methods had already been tried during wartime studies of inaccessible countries, inaccessible because the United States was at war with them. Now, though hostilities had ended, other countries and groups had become inaccessible. In the case of the Soviet Union and later Communist China, there were barriers to travel and research. In some cases, societies no longer existed— Jewish villages of Eastern Europe, for instance, whose survivors were scattered all over the world. Other cultures were being drastically altered by revolutionary changes, as in Indonesia and Thailand.

In the spring of 1947, Columbia University Research in Contemporary Cultures, made possible by a large Office of Naval Research grant for basic research in human behavior, was started under the directorship of Ruth Benedict. Margaret Mead became research director of the project, and she was also coconvener, with Geoffrey Gorer, of the Russian group, and a member of the French group besides. In all, seven cultures were chosen for study: pre-Soviet Great Russian, Polish, Czech, Chinese, French, Syrian, Eastern-European Jewish. RCC, as the project came to be known, employed the talents and labors of about 120 people, though not all worked at the same time, and included, as Margaret Mead later described them, "gifted people who had somehow managed in wartime, but who did not fit into the peacetime mold—the aberrant, the unsystemic, the people with work habits too irregular ever to hold regular jobs." Space for the project was meager and scattered: one room in the Columbia Department of Anthropology, one room in the office of the cultural counselor to the French consulate, three rooms at the Kips Bay Yorkville District Health Center, corners of Dr. Benedict's office at Columbia, and increasingly large portions of Dr. Mead's office at the American Museum of Natural History.

While anthropological interviewing of members of the culture being studied was probably the most important research method used, many other methods—the analysis of literature, films, documents, folklore, and graphic art—were also important in these studies of culture "at a distance." But for Margaret Mead the methods were valuable to the extent that they led to the important goal of helping the anthropologist to see the culture he wanted to learn about as represented and living in the organization of the individual personality.

In May of 1948, when RCC was well underway, Dr. Benedict was invited to go to a UNESCO (United Nations Educational, Scientific, Cultural Organization) seminar in Czechoslovakia, which would give her a chance to be in many of the countries she had worked on for many years "at a distance." Although her health had not been good for several years, she wanted very much to go. And so her friends, among them Dr. Mead, said, "Go! If this is what you want to do, do it." For this is what she had always said to her students during her teaching years. Two days after she returned from her trip she had a coronary thrombosis and was taken to the hospital. She lived only five days more. She was 61 when she died. Years later, in a book Margaret Mead wrote about Ruth Benedict, *An Anthropologist at Work*, she described seeing her just after her death. ". . . she looked incredibly old as if the wisdom and suffering of several hundred years was momentarily expressed in a face. She had always felt so strongly about the beauty of the dead, and we brought our children to see her, giving them a protection which few children have today, in an acceptance that death is a part of life."

Margaret Mead took over the directorship of RCC. She was now one of the few senior anthropologists who, in many ways, embodied the teaching of Franz Boas about anthropology and fieldwork. Younger anthropologists and students now looked to her for counseling and training.

The role of teacher was a natural one for Dr. Mead. She had spent the summers of 1945 and 1946 lecturing at the Vassar Summer Institute and had given the Jacob Gimbel lectures on the psychology of sex at Stanford University and the University of California. In 1947 she had lectured at Sèvres, France, at the UNESCO Workshop for International Understanding; and at the Harvard Seminar in American Civilization, in Salzburg, Austria, where Cathy went with her. In the fall of 1947 she began to lecture regularly at Teachers College, part of Columbia University. In 1952 she became a guest professor of anthropology at Columbia's School of General Studies, and after a year spent far away from New York City, once again among the Manus peoples of the Admiralty Islands in the Pacific, she returned to become in 1954, Adjunct Professor of Anthropology at Columbia University, a position she still holds.

Dr. Mead's classes were soon famous for being lively. She was known to be a strong and vital teacher, for she was able to bring even the most complex anthropological material to life through the endless examples she could draw upon from her field experiences. She often acted them out in the native language of whatever culture she happened to be discussing and almost always touched them with her own very special kind of humor. She had "the gift," as one graduate student put it, "of being able to capture the thing that everyone knows but rarely says. She can say it in a few words. She hits at the very human truth which is familiar, but which has never been said. And somehow that's very funny. It's not a joke—but it makes you feel warm." "Her enthusiasm catches you up," said another Ph.D. candidate. Students came to know that no matter how busy she was, in the brief time she had to give she was fully concerned with individual problems and needs. She was positive, encouraging, and she managed to communicate an expectation that her students *would* do well, that she had faith in their capacities. At the same time she was known to demand as much of her students as she did of herself, which meant a very great deal indeed. Students had to learn not to flinch beneath her very direct but always constructive criticisms.

She was no less critical, after all, with the American public, who had come to depend on her sharp analyses of their own culture. She published another book, *Male and Female: A Study of the Sexes in a Changing World,* in 1949. This time she compared what she had come to consider the basic essential differences between the sexes, the physical inheritance and common sexual experiences of men and women everywhere, with the social forms the two sexes adopted in the seven different Pacific Island cultures she had studied. And she put great emphasis, a quarter of the book in fact, on the more or less common experiences of the two sexes in "our complex American culture"—their childhoods, the ways they dated and courted, the attitudes towards sex and achievement they received from adults and from the books and magazines and

movies they saw, the kind of marriages they made. She ruth-
lessly analyzed the popular imagery of the day, pointed to
many ways in which American parents and makers of the
status quo forced young males and females to fit into molds
in which they were often uncomfortable and frequently
suffered—the way, for instance, a little girl in America is
taught *not* to behave like a boy, *not* to be a tomboy, while a
little boy is taught *not* to play with dolls, *not* to run away from
fights; or a woman is brought up to believe it is permissible for
her to faint and weep, and a man is made to understand that
those are things he must not do. Once again Margaret Mead
urged, as she had before in *Sex and Temperament,* that men and
women in the modern world discard rigid social definitions of
masculinity and femininity and accept the challenge of being
their full male and female selves in their own ways.

The value of what anthropologists had learned about human beings from human beings was widely recognized in postwar years, and Dr. Mead found the understandings she had
gained in primitive societies were increasingly in demand. In
the summer of 1948 she was asked to help formulate a new approach to mental health when the Third International Mental
Health Congress met in London. Because psychiatrists,
who had till then been mostly alone in dealing with problems of mental health illness, now realized how many of the
mental problems they found in their patients grew out of the
environment in which they lived, they had invited members of
many sciences and professions, sociologists, biologists,
anthropologists, and nurses, to participate. Anthropologists
who had witnessed ". . . the comparative wholeness of human beings . . . in some primitive communities" were specially
conscious of how the "fragmented complicated conditions of

modern life" as well as the rapidly changing nature of modern society had steadily put more strain on human beings. These factors, plus new recognitions: "the world is one, man is one biological species . . . the mental health of the statesmen and leaders of the world can be crucial—the importance of the statement in the UNESCO charter that 'Wars begin in the minds of men,' " prompted the Third International Mental Health Congress to adopt a world approach to mental health. As Dr. Mead said in Berlin in 1956, the Congress is dedicated to the pursuit of "a wholeness for human beings," since "No individual, no family, no voluntary group, no nation, can be whole today without a relationship to the emerging wholeness of the human race on this planet."

Dr. Mead attended many meetings and conferences on mental health in the following years. In 1956 she was president of the World Federation for Mental Health, in 1958 she helped direct a special conference on the family in Asia, and in 1961 a second International Study Group was convened by the World Federation for Mental Health at Roffey Park in England to take a new look at mental health from an international point of view. Because she had taken part in the 1948 meeting, she was able to see how much a world mental health point of view had been able to contribute to "millions of people, whole nations, generations to come," and how important it was to keep the focus of that point of view on the individual. "Only by keeping this emphasis on the individual," she wrote in the *American Journal of Orthopsychiatry*, a professional journal, in 1962, "on the effects on the individual, on the consequences for the individual, can we preserve a human perspective and the faith and the willingness to take the necessary action." Margaret Mead reaffirmed the value of the psychiatrist, the social worker, the teacher who must, she said, never lose their awareness of each and every one.

The growth and development and value of individual identity was also at the core of her concern for and participation with the young. Whether her work or writings or lectures had to do with the feeding of infants, the existing setup in America's schools, the training of teachers, the struggles of adolescents to find their place in a world of confused and shifting values, Dr. Mead saw the emerging of whole identities as the goal for which to strive.

In *Growth and Culture,* a photographic study of Balinese children published in 1951, which she wrote with Frances Cooke Macgregor with photographs by Gregory Bateson, she looked again at "the general problem of the way in which culture patterns human growth, emphasizing some potentialities and muting others. . . ." Her opening chapter defined the present time as "an age of awareness" in which she considered it a "moral imperative" for conscious adults to be aware of the extraordinary complexity of the life a newborn child will have to live. Awareness, she thought, could be most telling in the area of early child development where extreme sensitivity to the growth process and the way in which the culture is expressed in a particular child might make the difference between wholeness and something much less sound. The photographs in the book, which showed Balinese children in varying activities, postures, and relationships, and the accompanying text related the visual images to the cultural descriptions so clearly that the reader could not help but become aware.

Whenever Dr. Mead addressed groups of teachers, a part of what she had to say to them always included how vital it was for them to remain flexible, to continue to grow, to be able to learn from their pupils, and above all to make each child in their classes feel his or her own individuality and essential-ness. While she lectured to teachers in Tasmania, Australia, in 1951, her daughter Cathy, now eleven, "studied" Australian schools. Dr. Mead asked teachers—in Australia and every-where—to try, despite the many burdens they bore of over-crowded classrooms and difficult teaching situations, to kindle the spark of originality and enthusiasm that crops up in a child so often, when, perhaps, "after he's been reading bad poetry for months, somebody by accident put a good poem in his reader. So a child," said Dr. Mead, "with enormous excite-ment starts reading 'Tiger, Tiger, burning bright' and jumps out of his seat and begins to roar. Now most teachers don't en-courage that at all, and say 'James, sit down!' Under those cir-cumstances, that child may decide that nothing that's ever go-ing to happen in that school matters again, and he will never see the image of a tiger hard enough to want to roar any more. He will simply learn things on the edge of his mind, and he will not learn about tigers that are bright, and orange and beau-tiful, and roaring—in a forest; he will learn t-i-g-e-r. That'll please teachers that don't like people to roar when they hear about tigers. There'll never be any tigers any more—just words out of a spelling book." It is questionable how many teachers in her audience were capable of stepping this far into a child's world.

Concern for the schools and teachers of the United States gave rise to a small book, *The School in American Culture,* actually the text of an Inglis lecture she had given at Harvard University, in which Dr. Mead talked about what she consid-ered to be the biggest task of the teacher of today. This was the job of trying to teach "unknown" children. They are "un-known" because they live in a world that is changing so rapidly that they are not only strangers in many respects to their own parents—who grew up in a very different, and in many ways a more stable world—but a difficult challenge to the teacher. The teacher herself, born and brought up in a world of the past like their parents, is expected to conduct into the future children of a world in many ways alien to her, in which the science fiction of her childhood has become the reality of her pupils' present. What should such teachers do? Try in many ways to keep close to the changing world of the young students and help them remain close to themselves. For "Only by steadily projecting our vision forward," she wrote in a later pamphlet, "Understanding the Child," concerning the same problem, "while we keep our observation finely attuned to the needs and fears and hopes of these new children . . . can we hope to provide the conditions of growth for the next generation who might deal with problems too vast for us . . . even to think about properly . . ." But because she was always able to identify closely with the members of any generation, she recognized the price that many of the children of the mid-twentieth century were paying "for this new flexibility, this new awareness, this new capacity to shift and change, to pause and weigh," which was, she said, "the price of loneliness . . . come with learning to live all alone in a series of changing new worlds."

The whole question of how quickly human beings can change and adapt to change seemed to Margaret Mead to be the most pressing problem to investigate. She had already decided in 1951 that it was again time for cultural anthropologists like herself "to go back to our laboratories in the jungles, on the small islands, around the arctic fringes of the world." Some of her anthropologist friends in Australia persuaded her to go back to see what had happened on the island of Manus in the 25 years since she last had been there. She decided that perhaps these peoples whom she had studied as children a quarter of a century ago, and who in the interim had been part of the battle-ground of a World War, and had experienced two occupations —first by the Japanese, then by the Americans—perhaps the Manus whom she had once known quite well might provide clues to understanding other changing cultures and societies. For from what she had heard, it seemed that the Manus had changed so drastically and so unaccountably that they had moved in one generation from the Stone Age into the complex present. From nearly naked savages who believed in magic and made war with spears they had moved to become potential members of the modern world, as she later described them in her book, *New Lives for Old*, "with ideas of boundaries in time and space, responsibility to God, enthusiasm for law, and committed to trying to build a democratic community, edu-cate their children, police and landscape their village, care for the old and the sick, and erase age-old hostilities with neigh-bouring tribes."

The second trip to Manus in 1953 reflected great changes in the life of an anthropologist as well. Dr. Mead returned to the Admiralties by plane, not on a ship, bringing with her all kinds of valuable new equipment: fine cameras, sensitive lenses, tape recorders, high-speed films, testing equipment, new medicines. Two young fieldworkers, Ted Schwartz, who had done his graduate work at the University of Pennsylvania, and his wife, an art student trained in fieldwork, went with her to Manus.

The old village of Peri, built on water, was gone, aban-doned forever during the war, and in its place, constructed on land, Margaret Mead found a new village, row upon row of

"American-style" houses all of the same design, not quite as beautiful or as suitable to meet the periodic gales as the old thatched arched houses had been. The people of Manus, who had been told that Piyap, "Woman of the West," was coming back to them, were overjoyed to see her once more. So much had happened since her departure. They had never written to her—almost no one could write. And now, once again, she, who had known them in the days before the "new movement," who could see and appreciate what they had done, and who had cared enough to remember them all this time—she was to be among them once more. They enjoyed seeing the old photographs of themselves that she had taken in 1928. One said: "We had forgotten all these things, these houses, these faces, and now you bring the photographs and they all come back. And where were they all these years? In your photographs. We had lost them."

For Dr. Mead the return was also a new and amazing experience. There, grown-up and tall and many of them leaders of their villages, were the boys who had worked in her house in 1928—John Kilipak, Loponiu, Kapeli—who now called her "Mama" and dressed in carefully pressed white suits. Still alive were some of the older men like Pokanau, who had never believed he would see her again, and could talk over with her the old days now described as "Ol stink fasin bilong ol big fela man bilong bipo," which loosely translated meant, "all the stinking ways of the big men of before."

She had not been in Manus long before she found herself deluged with questions: What is the best way to run a school? Is this medicine a good one for the children? A few minutes after her arrival the first night, she had been handed a letter by the man who was the present locally chosen school teacher and whom she had known as a little child. The letter read: "Dear Missus Markrit: This letter is to ask you whether you will help me teach the children." In that moment and others that followed, faced with a people who came to her with written down rules and documents and notes "written by people whom one had never visualized as becoming part of the modern world, with whom, in truth, there had been no hope of real two-way communication. . . . I felt almost as if someone—and I was not quite sure who it was, they or I—had been raised from the dead. Someone who, not knowing it, had been dead and lived again." The word *literacy* became real to her as it had never been before.

A week had not gone by after their arrival when Dr. Mead in Peri and the Schwartzes in Bunai, a village some two miles away, found themselves living, quite literally on the edge of a volcano. A volcano that had not been there when they came had appeared suddenly out of the sea—first as a column of steam, then as a series of explosions in the night. Further evidence of the volcano's reality appeared the next morning in the form of black pumice that covered the surrounding sea for miles. The Australian administration sent a police boy running across the island to tell Dr. Mead, her assistants, and the coastal villagers that they must evacuate their dwellings and move at once to higher land. The crisis, which meant packing and unpacking and moving to an unhealthy mosquito-infested group of ramshackle houses on the top of a small mountain, also had its happy aspect for Dr. Mead, who profited, she felt, from being able to see how the new Manus acted in time of emergency. Before they decided to return to their own villages and take their chances with the volcano, she watched them hold democratically run meetings in which everyone had his chance to speak his mind until finally an orderly vote was taken.

On her return to the village of Peri, Margaret Mead settled down in the house she had been given, and which she found perfectly located for watching—it was in the dead center of the village on the town square. Her house was open to everyone, always full of people, and she had a veranda on which the children played—all very much as it had been in 1928. Again she was soon deeply involved in village life. She ran a dispensary and trained members of the village to bandage and dress sores. She helped take care of the children. The Manus felt free to come to her at any time of the day or night with a problem. What was different, however, was that the new Manus were able to help her too, for they had become very verbal, concerned with record keeping—a trait dear to Dr. Mead's heart—and extremely conscious of the fact that it was important for her to learn how fast a people can change, and that what they had done was significant for the rest of the world. "Remember," said Samol, leader of one of the villages, to his council, "that for these months everything you do will be recorded, filmed, put on tape . . . and *all America* will know whether we are succeeding in our new way of life."

In the 25 years that had passed, Margaret Mead's work schedule had not slackened; if anything it had become more strenuous. Up early every morning, she spent the days collecting her information by notes, photographs, on tape. Late at night when the village grew quiet she would type up the day's notes, taken in a sort of shorthand and directly in pidgin English, till one or two in the morning. At the end of six months in Manus she had three fat volumes of condensed notes typed on both sides of each sheet. "She accomplishes," said Dr.

[*174*]

Schwartz, who was amazed at her output, "in six months what takes most fieldworkers one or two years." The only "break" she had in months came when she was called to answer a telephone call from the United States. To reach the telephone took a whole day's sea-voyage by canoe. The ocean was very rough —Dr. Mead cannot swim—the trip meant precious time away from her work. When she got to the telephone and the connection was made with America, she was asked by some bright man in an advertising firm: "What cigarette do you smoke?"

The changes wrought in the Manus way of life were deep and authentic, as Margaret Mead learned. They stemmed, she believed, to a great extent from the fact that the Manus had always been a people dependent, as fishermen and seafarers, on their contacts with other peoples and other ways of life. They had frequently changed or adapted inventions from their consciousness of others. Then the many foreign influences they had known—German till 1914, Australian from 1914 to the present, the Japanese occupation from 1942 to 1944, and the American occupation from 1944 till the end of the war—had helped to prepare them for the big changes that they themselves brought about when the war was over. They had decided to convert to Christianity in the early 1930's because they felt that the white man's wealth and power must be somehow connected with the white man's religion; therefore it had to be a better religion than their own. Now when the war came, they were very sensitive to all the gadgets and machinery and methods of organization they encountered, particularly those of the Americans, whom they felt closest to. When they were once more free to live their own lives, they made their great cultural transition in a short space of time, constructing a systematic society out of the bits and pieces of the white man's life they knew and admired. A strong and imaginative man named Paliau, the man who, as Dr. Mead phrased it, "met the hour," was the leader of the "new movement." They tried to put into practice the whole set of the white man's institutions, schools, hospitals, courts.

Yes, what she had found in Manus had great and positive meaning for the United States and for the world; and Margaret Mead felt reassured that the necessity or decision to change quickly did not necessarily spell disaster, doom, or badly damaged personalities. Though much of what was occurring in the greater world beyond Manus—the need to cope with nuclear energy, mounting populations, the pressures of the emerging underdeveloped areas of Africa and Asia—was almost overwhelming for the human race, she had seen one group of human beings who had changed themselves almost completely, jumped thousands of years in only a few, taken "a cultural giant step," and emerged the stronger for it. Perhaps, she reasoned, the slow approach to change favored generally by Western countries was not as wise as the fast approach the Manus had used; for the Manus had transformed themselves quickly enough to be able to see and enjoy their own transformation. That the Manus had wanted to change, been ready to change, and had changed all together were also, she felt, significant factors.

New Lives for Old, published in 1956, "the record of a people who have moved faster than any people of whom we have records," was offered by Dr. Mead "as food for the imagination of Americans, whom the people of Manus so deeply admire." And if, at a moment when Americans were faced with the possibility of nuclear war, the end of civilization, the end of the human race, despair was possible, she hoped the American people might take courage from the story of the Manus, who believed, even if many Americans had forgotten it, in the America that was built on change—and that was always new "because the men who built it have themselves incorporated the ability to change. . . ." "This precious quality," wrote Dr. Mead in the introduction to the book, "which Americans have developed through three and a half centuries of beginning life, over and over, in a virgin land, is a belief that man can learn and change—quickly, happily, without violence, without madness, without coercion, and of their own free will."

Chapter 12

Margaret Mead—Today and Tomorrow

Margaret Mead's farewell to Manus in 1953 was not a last good-bye. N G A I, mysterious letters on a few drawers of a file cabinet in her office stand for New Guinea Admiralty Islands—her next big anthropological venture. This five-year project will take her back to Manus and to other of the Admiralty Islands in 1964, and back into the interior of New Guinea as well. Dr. Ted Schwartz, her co-worker in Manus in 1953, field director of this project with the help of his anthropologist wife, Dr. Lola Romanucci Schwartz, went out to start the work in 1963. Dr. Mead expects to join them every summer.

The new study is to be in two parts: the first will concentrate on determining what factors shaped the various cultures existing in the Admiralty Islands and how the various cultures have affected each other's development. In New Guinea, the second part of the job will be, first, to find a primitive, still untouched people, probably in the Upper Sepik region, an area still unknown to Dr. Mead, so that the anthropologists may have yet one more chance to study the inner structure of a really primitive society, one of the last to exist in a nuclear age. Once such a group has been found, Margaret Mead, who began her field work in 1923, will, after all of 40 years of experience, with the aid of all the modern devices at her disposal and in the light of new questions that need answering, look again—and look for one of the last times in the history of the human race—at primitive man and his Stone Age culture. The anthropological problem will be a classical one: the study of the structure of a society. But whatever she and Dr. Schwartz and the other anthropologists learn there will be useful and perhaps crucially important in helping contemporary man to live in his own highly complicated present-day society and in the still unknown societies of the future.

The sense of continuity—so important to Dr. Mead even in her childhood when she worried about the boats floating down the river (with perhaps no one to bring them ashore)— and of the importance of passing on traditions, that sense is with her still. It pervades every area of her work and life. In 1958 she returned to Bali with photographer Ken Heyman to see and photograph again the babies she had studied in the 1930's just before World War II, babies now grown up and with babies of their own. She is still in touch with peoples in the many cultures she has studied. The work begun in so many different fields—mental health, child development, education —has expanded and grown, and she is more actively involved in all of them than ever.

The Mead family tradition now extends from the past into the future. Mary Catherine Bateson, her daughter Cathy, is now also Mrs. Barkev Kassarjian, with her own doctorate as a linguist specializing in the Middle East. She is the fourth generation of women in her family to go into the social sciences, and she is following her mother's belief that a woman should have a separate professional identity, whether or not she is married. Her father and mother were divorced soon after World War II, but the separation involved no break in Catherine's relationship to both parents; and she shares her mother's belief that in a society where marriage is terminable and marriages within a profession are especially fragile, the parents of a child still retain a relationship to one another. So Catherine's father gave her away at her wedding and stood beside her mother at the reception. The wedding was a ritual high point for her widely scattered family.

As Cathy grew up, she was permitted, as her mother had been, to make her own choices. At the age of 15, she went to France, lived with a French family, and learned the language. At 16, she went to Israel with her mother, who was a consultant for the Israeli government, and decided to stay and finish high school in Israel, thus adding Hebrew to her repertoire of languages. When she returned to the United States, she went to Radcliffe College in Cambridge, Massachusetts, began as a freshman to study Arabic, and decided to specialize in Middle Eastern languages. Among the languages she has studied is Armenian, the first language of her husband, a social scientist engineer born in Syria, whom she met while in college.

Still another recurrent theme out of Margaret Mead's own childhood emerges in the wooded place in Hancock, New Hampshire, recently bought by the Kassarjians. Dr. Mead has always believed every child ought to have a country landscape that is familiar to him and that will remain throughout his life as a "point of reference—for writing and thinking, for remembering and imagining." In her own childhood there had been, of course, the five acres on the edge of Hammonton, New Jersey, then, later, the 107-acre farm in Bucks County, Pennsylvania. When Cathy was little, her "country" had been the country place of the Lawrence K. Franks, Cloverly, in Holderness, New Hampshire, where Margaret Mead had often joined her to take part in conferences and in the summer intellectual life that centered on the Franks. And the New Hampshire lakes and hills had been Cathy's country point of reference, just as "the sandy pine woods with winter green and arbutus of New Jersey and the wooded soft valleys of Pennsylvania" had been for her mother.

Now, when her crowded schedule permits, Margaret Mead will go to New Hampshire to visit her daughter and son-in-law —to breathe mountain air, to walk in the woods, to rest, but also perhaps to work with her young colleagues, as her daughter and son-in-law may now be called. Mary Catherine Bateson recently edited the proceedings of a conference for which her mother wrote the concluding chapter, and is working actively as a linguist, integrating the interest in nonverbal communication that rests partly on the work that her father, Gregory Bateson, and her mother did in Bali. Her son-in-law J. B. Kassarjian, Catherine's husband, who has been specializing in small group conference processes, accompanied Margaret Mead to a conference on world settlement patterns held on a ship in Greek waters in the summer of 1963.

So the circle has come round. For Dr. Mead thinks of her work as being in some ways divided into three periods: the first in which she learned from those older than herself, Professor Boas, Ruth Benedict, William F. Ogburn, Edward Sapir, Radcliffe Brown, Lawrence K. Frank; the second, when she worked mostly with people of her own age group and as half of a husband-and-wife team in the field; and the third, the present, in which she finds herself working increasingly with those a decade or two or three decades younger than herself. One of her younger co-workers is now her daughter, who is also helping bring ashore some of the boats Margaret Mead launched years ago.

Today Margaret Mead is probably busier than she has ever been in all of her tremendously busy life. She may be the busiest woman in the world; she is certainly one of them. For she carries the multiplied responsibilities of being a woman who has come to know a great deal about many important matters, and who is therefore very much needed and in demand. Her many interests, like seeds planted in fertile ground, have all taken root, grown, and blossomed, leaving Dr. Mead in the midst of a fruitful but somewhat overwhelming garden that needs constant tending.

As Associate Curator at the American Museum of Natural History, she is preparing a set of three-dimensional exhibits, for the new Hall, Peoples of the Pacific, that will be revolutionary; for they are designed to allow film and television cameras to photograph from all sides. Her teaching schedule now includes about 250 lectures a year, 60 of them as Adjunct Professor of Anthropology to Columbia graduate students who take her courses. (She reads and grades all her students' papers herself.) She is a visiting lecturer in the Department of Psychiatry at the University of Cincinnati and Visiting Professor of Anthropology at the Menninger School of Psychiatry in Topeka, Kansas. She serves as a consultant to colleges, universities, and school systems throughout the United States and abroad on all kinds of questions, ranging from curriculum to social life to integration. Business, management, governments seek her advice. She is studying attitudes toward time and space and the image of the scientist with Dr. Rhoda Metraux, a close friend and colleague with whom she shares a four-story house in Greenwich Village. She travels and lectures for the World Federation of Mental Health. She speaks for and to all kinds of organizations, especially those concerned with problems of child development and human well-being and of family life. Recently, she spoke at a dinner of Parents Without Partners, an organization of divorced parents, discussing the difficulties facing the "nuclear family"; at a governors' conference in Illinois, she spoke about youth; at a governors' conference in New York, she spoke on aging. She attends innumerable conferences, addresses many commencement classes. In June of 1963, at Lincoln University in Pennsylvania, she spoke about integration, and told her audience that though "We have condemned generations of children of some groups to cultural and economic deprivation . . . the ferment that exists all over the nation today is not because we are a backward and bigoted nation, but because we are not, and because we let change develop within a free society."

She continues to do research on contemporary peoples of complex modern societies because she believes that "If communication and understanding is ever to be free and open, the peoples of the world must comprehend each other's social systems and cultural patterns." She considers the struggle for world peace "the major task of our time," and for this reason works with the National Committee for a Gradual Approach to Peace, the Scientists' Institute for Public Information, and is on the Advisory Council of the Peace Research Institute. In

February of 1963, she attended the United Nations Conference on the Application of Science and Technology for the Benefit of Less Developed Areas, which met in Geneva, Switzerland, to try to find ways of dealing with the gigantic job of feeding, housing, and educating a world population that was estimated to reach something like 6,000,000,000 people by the year 2000. And looking ahead to other problems, she is concerned with trying to understand the creative process, the challenge of increased leisure, new situations created by space travel, probing deeper into questions of individuality.

On all of these subjects, and many others, she writes voluminously, as she always has. Words seem to flow miraculously from the small portable typewriter she prefers to use. She can write anywhere and does—on planes, trains, in taxicabs. She can write in small snatches of time, such as a few minutes between appointments, or in larger spans of an hour or two early in the morning before going to the office. A partial bibliography of her writings beginning with the year 1947 runs to nearly 30 pages. She has written 12 books and been coauthor and editor of 10 others, and has written an uncounted number of pamphlets, articles, and professional papers. She has been a regular contributor to *Redbook* magazine since December, 1961, and has answered questions there on such subjects as overpopulation, the school prayer issue, homosexuality, telepathy, happiness, sex on the campus, and college for women. She writes for other magazines—too many to name —and she is often written about.

She is constantly being interviewed by the press and frequently makes headlines. She is widely quoted on just about everything:

On American fathers: "Fathers are spending too much time taking care of babies. No other civilization ever let responsible and important men spend their time this way."

On juvenile delinquency: "It's going up all over the world, under every system. We've failed to organize our cities in such a way that the whole community takes responsibility for its children."

On museums: "I think all museums should be directed toward 12-year-old boys. They're the brightest group you can find and this is the age when you can arouse their curiosity and interest."

On junior high school: "Junior high school seemed like a fine idea when we invented it, but it turned out to be an invention of the devil. We're catching our boys in a net for which they're socially unprepared. We put them in junior high school with girls who are about two years ahead of them. There isn't a thing they should have to do with girls at this age except growl at them."

How any one human being can, like an infinitely competent juggler, keep so many balls in the air without dropping any is a mystery even to her office staff, an indefinite number of intelligent young women who try to assist Dr. Mead in the monumental tasks she has set herself. The same niche, hidden away in the southwest tower of the American Museum of Natural History, still serves as her office, though it has been greatly changed in the more than 35 years that have elapsed since young Margaret Mead, just back from Samoa, first moved into it. In place of the bare walls on which she found room to hang a Samoan tapa, though the office now consists of three rooms instead of the original one, there is not a square inch of space. File cabinets, bookcases, desks, cartons, all crammed with papers, fieldnotes, letters, photos, and books. books, books (many by Margaret Mead) fill every corner. On her desk, the same one she has always worked at, are various objects given to her by friends or brought back from the field, among them a model Japanese rice baby and a Balinese carving. On the glass doors of the big cabinets facing her, which house most of her writings, are many photographs, most of them of her daughter Catherine at various ages.

This is the center of the hurricane, where the mail comes in—mountains of it—from everywhere. There is no time to answer the letters, but they are answered—every one of them— sooner or later. There are many, many requests for her to speak or write; letters from scientists and colleagues about work, from friends, often anthropologists, in distant countries, from relatives, from some of the men and women she has known in the then primitive societies she studied; a constant barrage of questions from everyone—mothers worried about their children, older people with burdens of illness or loneliness or retirement, young men and women having troubles in love and marriage, children—even little ones—with problems they find big, and which Margaret Mead takes just as seriously. All are answered. She even took the time to reply to a young woman who asked her for her favorite recipe.

The telephones ring almost constantly in Margaret Mead's office. When she is there and not absorbed in serious writing or some other urgent work, she speaks in her deep, strong voice that says exactly what it means to many people in a day. Sometimes her concern is to help a student or young anthropologist or social scientist be placed where he can do the research he wants to do. Sometimes she is busy trying to assist a friend in trouble. Sometimes visitors, mostly expected ones, find their way through the labyrinthine upper corridors of the Museum to her office. She sees several students regularly. There is always a group of students whose work she is supervising closely as they leave for the field or as they come back to write up their work. There is, for instance, a blind student who has just gone to study the blind in Mexican villages, two students who have just left for Pakistan, another who is just returning from New Guinea. At times an occasional child who has been given a class assignment to visit the famous anthropologist comes to call. She will give as much attention and consideration to an eighth grader come for an interview as she will to a reporter from the New York *Times* or to a colleague who has dropped in en route perhaps from Asia to Europe.

The young women who work for Dr. Mead try to keep the storm of activity under control. Her administrative assistant, a young Southern woman doing graduate work in anthropology, is in charge of Dr. Mead's "impossible schedule," and is responsible for seeing that MM, as she is known in memos and other interoffice communications, gets on and off planes and trains in time to be *where* she is supposed to be *when* she is supposed to be there. The rest of her staff, except for her course assistant, are called research assistants, and they do all kinds of jobs, including, of course, typing and secretarial chores. On days in the office when Dr. Mead is trying to do the undoable and expects everyone else to do the same, life is harrying. But Margaret Mead's young assistants feel the strain is well worth the good fortune of being able to work for "such an amazing woman." She is to them "a teacher, not a boss"—"a big person whose impatience is never personal." And they all fear that after working for Dr. Mead, any other job they might find would "have to be boring."

It might be easy to think of Margaret Mead as a woman so totally dedicated to her work that she may not seem quite real, or like the people one meets every day. But this, as anyone privileged enough to know her at all knows—her friends, her staff, her co-workers, or even authors writing about her—is far, far from the truth. For she is tremendously real. If she seems bigger in some ways than ordinary life, it is because she is so much in touch with everything she sees or comes in contact with that more life seems to come through her. One has only to read her own books and articles to discover her. Many people have not, and for them she is therefore only a photograph in a newspaper or someone seen on television. No one writing about Margaret Mead can bring her to life as well as she can herself in her own work. There a reader finds how the big world with which she is concerned is made up for her of many little details, each one of them real and important to her, none too small for her attention. She is aware of the ways a tiny child sees dandelions, or of how a little bowl or cup and spoon can give a baby a sense of his own world. (And so she can tell mothers and teachers important truths about bringing up children.) When working with primitive people, she is constantly alert to everything: the kind of leaves woven into a mat, the exact manner in which different members of the tribe dance. An anthropologist, after all, has to be *in touch*—his life may depend on knowing just where the crocodiles are.

In this way the big understandings that Margaret Mead has to offer to people throughout the world today have been made out of a myriad of smaller truths and understandings, concrete ones, which may be called reality. For Margaret

Mead is a realist, a woman who sees what exists, does not sentimentalize, has the courage to accept what *is* in the belief that only in that way can things be changed and made better. And she has great faith in change. She is also a teacher—not just to her students but for everyone to whom she speaks or writes—who understands the necessity for discipline and speed, who despises wasted time, admires accuracy, and wants her students not to be lazy or slovenly or "to bungle," but to hurry, hurry, hurry, because there is much to be done to meet that glorious inner vision she has of what the world and human beings might be.

She is also warm, and her sense of humor is world-famous. So are her tempers. She is a mature grown-up woman of over 60 in whom one senses at the same time the spirit of the little girl she must have been. She is a woman, very much a woman —not because she can cook and loves babies, which she does, but because of the loving, orderly, motherly spirit that is so much a part of her. She is a positive force who seems to command and help everyone who comes in contact with her to be one too.

Above all, she is a free and strong and original self, which makes her impossible to define or pigeonhole, and thus controversial to anyone who likes to label and limit the people around him. She was brought up to be free, and she is committed to the task of helping other human beings achieve that same freedom so that they too may be able to contribute their full talents and abilities to the world, a world so badly in need, she feels, of every individual gift, especially now when the very survival of the human race may depend on it.

Where is the source of Margaret Mead's strength? It is not, like Samson's in her hair, or like Atlas in his muscles. It is in her childhood, where, through the understanding and love of her parents, she first knew the joy of being alive and of being herself—free to choose, free to be. But Margaret Mead can say it better—much better.

Here is a poem she wrote at 21. It is about her childhood and, at the same time, about all childhoods.

Of So Great Glee

She used to skip when she was small
Till all her frocks were tattered,
But mother gently gathered up
The dishes that she shattered.

Her skipping rope got caught in trees
And shook their blossoms down,
But her laugh was so light-hearted
That the dryads could not frown.

And when at last she tore a star
Out of the starry sky,
God only smiled at one whose glee
Could fling a rope so high.

KEN HEYMAN: MAGNUM PHOTOS

[191]

Acknowledgments

I should like to give special thanks to Dr. Margaret Mead for allowing me to refer to and use passage from various of her reprinted articles and pamphlets, as well as from her private papers and unpublished manuscripts.

I owe also many personal thanks to Dr. Mead for her time and contribution to this book, and to her staff for their kindness and general assistance.

Allyn Moss

The editors would like to thank Dr. Mead for her patience and perseverance in working on the book at every stage and for her generous cooperation in providing illustrative materials. Any errors which may have persisted are to be charged to the editors' account.